Sang Thong

A DANCE-DRAMA FROM THAILAND

❀ Sang Thong

A DANCE-DRAMA ❀ ❀ ❀
FROM THAILAND   Written by
King Rama II & the Poets of His Court

Translation with Introduction & Notes
by FERN S. INGERSOLL

Illustrated by Bunson Sukhphun

Charles E. Tuttle Company
RUTLAND, VERMONT & TOKYO, JAPAN

895.91
P577a
1973

Representatives

For Continental Europe:
BOXERBOOKS, INC., *Zurich*
For the British Isles:
PRENTICE-HALL INTERNATIONAL, INC., *London*
For Australasia:
PAUL FLESCH & CO., PTY. LTD., *Melbourne*
For Canada:
M. G. HURTIG, LTD., *Edmonton*

This book is one of the volumes assisted by the Asian
Literature Program of the Asia Society, Inc. New York.

Published by the Charles E. Tuttle Company, Inc.
of Rutland, Vermont & Tokyo, Japan
with editorial offices at
Suido 1-chome, 2-6, Bunkyo-ku, Tokyo

Copyright in Japan, 1973
by Charles E. Tuttle Co., Inc.

Library of Congress Catalog Card No. 72-88097
International Standard Book No. 0-8048 1002-8

First printing, 1973

PRINTED IN JAPAN

For my Mother & Father

Table of Contents

List of Illustrations

Preface

This translation and study of the background and present-day importance of *Sang Thong* have been done in an effort to discover in a literary work expressions of Thai views of life, and especially of views that offer some contrast with those of the West; to trace some of *Sang Thong*'s motifs within the wider context of Southeast Asian and Indian patterns of thought; and to gain some insight into its dual historical development as it was gradually formulated by learned priests and refined courtiers, as well as by common, fun-loving villagers.

I have chosen for translation the dance-drama version of the Sang Thong story attributed to Phra Putthaloetla (King Rama II), the second king of the present Thai dynasty, who reigned in the early 19th century. This version is from *Bot Lakhon Nok Ruam 6 Rueang: Phrarach-aniphon Ratachakan II* [Scripts for Six Dance-Dramas in the Style of *Lakhon Nok,* by King Rama II et al.], published in Bangkok by the National Library in 1958.

In an effort to retain as much of the subtlety of Thai thought as is possible in English, I have translated the first act, "The Birth of Prince Sang," line by line, with explanatory notes. Although these notes are at the back of the text, they are (unlike citations) an integral part of my effort in this translation to understand the Thai mind. Reflections of the Indian tradition in the characters and imagery of *Sang Thong* also appear in these notes. The remaining eight acts I have summarized with notes, again trying to preserve non-Western images and expressions reflecting values which historically or currently have been part of Thai life.

Illustrations for "The Birth of Prince Sang" were done by Bunson Sukhphun, who has lived all his life in the Thai rice village where our family lived for a year. He feels his court scenes lay no claim to period authenticity, but show what is in the minds of many country and city Thais when they recall the Sang Thong story. The country scenes illustrate in accurate detail the way of life during his boyhood some twenty years ago, which in many respects resembles rural life as it existed in the period of Rama II and as it continues even today.

ON TRANSLITERATION

Writing Thai words in Western script has, through the years, followed a variety of systems, no one of which is right for all purposes. I have basically followed the system recommended by the Library of Congress, which is not greatly different from that devised by the Royal Institute of Thailand. Stated briefly,

The vowels *a, e, i, o, u* are pronounced as in Italian.

th (as in Thai) sounds like *t* as in "top"
ph (as in Phanthurat) sounds like *p* as in "pin"
kh (as in *lakhon*) sounds like *k* as in "king"
k (as in *klon*) sounds like *g* as in "go"

In the words *Sang Thong, lakhon nok,* and *klon,* the *o* has the sound of *aw* as in "dawn."

For students of linguistics or of the Thai language the system may be summarized in somewhat more detail:

Voiced stops (initial position only)	*b, d*
Voiceless, unaspirated stops	*p, t, ch, k*
Voiceless, aspirated stops	*ph, th, ch, kh*
Voiceless spirants	*f, s, h*
Voiced nasals	*m, n, ng*
Front unrounded vowels	*i, e, ae*
Central unrounded vowels	*ue, oe, a*
Back rounded vowels	*u, o, aw*
Voiced semivowels—initial position	*y, w*
Voiced semivowels—final position	*i, o* (after *a, ae*)
	w (after *i*)

Except in the cases of *Sang Thong, lakhon nok,* and *klon,* mentioned above, which have previously appeared in English-language publications about Thai theater, I have used *aw* as in "dawn" to represent the third back-rounded vowel. I have also substituted *likay,* a form which appears in earlier English-language publications, for *like.*

I have used the conventional spelling for proper names.

For Pali words, I have used a generally accepted system of transliteration.

Acknowledgments

Having tried to understand a drama embedded in a culture which is not my own, I owe debts of gratitude to many people who have guided me through an unfamiliar web of thoughts, feelings, and styles of expression. However, if I have at times become entangled in the web, it was through no fault of my patient guides.

I would like to thank Dean Rong Sayamanonda and M. L. Chirayu Navawongs, who made possible my studies of Thai literature at Chulalongkorn University, Bangkok. M. L. Chirayu directed me to Professor Vacharee Ramyanandand, who suggested Sang Thong *as an expression of Thai views and values and then spent many hours helping me to understand it. Mrs. Buaphan Potaya and Mrs. Pratoom Ganjing also helped me with translation and explanations of ideas behind the words. Mrs. Maenmas Chavalit, head librarian of the National Library of Thailand, critically checked the translation of Act One and its explanatory notes, offering many perceptive interpretations.*

For a varied insight into Thai culture, I am indebted to the late Phya Anuman Rajadhon, who was my teacher for intermittent periods during the last fifteen years. Professor Visudh Busyakul made many of the Pali and Sanskrit sources of Thai literature meaningful to me. Later, at Catholic University, Dr. Siegfried A. Schulz offered suggestions helpful in further understanding Indian contributions to Sang Thong, *and Dr. John Brown critically read the manuscript from the perspective of comparative literature.*

Dr. Samrit Khunmuang brought me much of the information I have on Sang Thong *in Laos, after appointments with knowledgeable Laotians were arranged by Mr. Louis Connick, representative of the Asia Foundation.*

I would like to express my appreciation to Mr. Dhanit Yupho, retired director-general of the Fine Arts Department of Thailand, and to Mr. Montri Tramod, Miss Charuay Raksabhongsa, and Mrs. La-iad Herabataya of the School of Fine Arts for their explanations of the staging of Thai lakhon nok, *and to Professor Khomkhai Nilprapassorn of Chulalongkorn University for her background information on the development of varied forms of Thai drama.*

When the web of Thai culture has seemed particularly intricate, I have felt special gratitude toward Mrs. Somai Siphadung and numerous other Thais who kept Sang Thong, *as it is loved by people in the Thai countryside, a real part of life for me. At these times my husband, Jasper Ingersoll, with whom I have long shared an interest in Thai views of the world, was constantly helpful with suggestions and critical comments.*

I would also like to thank the publishers for permission to quote a passage from page 22 of Myth and Reality, *by Mircea Eliade, translated by Willard R. Trask (New York: Harper and Row, 1963).*

Finally, the encouragement of Mrs. Bonnie Crown of the Asia Society's Asian Literature Program has made possible this effort to understand something of Thai cultural character as it is expressed in this one delightful segment of its literary heritage.

Introduction

When *Sang Thong* (The Golden Prince of the Conch Shell) is mentioned in Thailand, people respond with wamth and enthusiasm; an elderly villager will describe with relish traveling players' performances he has often seen; a taxi driver will speak of the verses he studied in the fourth grade; a young working-girl in Bangkok will describe one act she recently saw performed when she visited the place where the guardian spirit of the city resides; a professor will relate her feeling of delight as she reread *Sang Thong* to write notes for a student edition.

Although numerous versions of *Sang Thong* exist, students read and actors (to varying degrees) follow the dance-drama form written by King Rama II and the poets of his court during the first quarter of the 19th century. Yet the centuries-old plot is well known to many people in Thailand, in the villages and in the countryside, who have not read *Sang Thong* in this or any other version.

HISTORY: INTERACTION OF A "GREAT" AND
A "LITTLE" TRADITION

The flow of ideas between a "great" tradition (perpetuated by temples and courts) and a "little" tradition (perpetuated by the common people) and back again to the "great" tradition is apparent in the history of the oral and written versions of the Sang Thong story.[1] So old and widespread in Southeast Asia is this basic story, however, that it is impossible to trace its origin. From amid the currents set in motion by migrations, religious missions, and trade expeditions, and by the conquering forces that have crossed Southeast Asia for centuries, few facts can be established with certainty, though more can be reasonably surmised.

Beginnings: The Golden Shell Birth-Story

The earliest written version of the Sang Thong story in Thailand was a story called "Suvarna-Sankha-Jātaka" (Golden Shell Birth-Story) in the *Pannāsa Jātaka,* a collection of fifty stories of the lives of the Buddha before the incarnation in which he achieved enlightenment.[2] Sometime between A.D. 1400 and 1600, according to the Thai historian Prince Damrong, a Buddhist priest or group of priests in Chiang Mai (now northern Thailand) collected and wrote the stories in the *Pannāsa Jātaka.*[3]

At that time priests from Chiang Mai commonly went to study in Ceylon, where the *Nipāta Jātaka,* part of the

Pali canon,[4] was well known and highly respected. This *Nipāta Jātaka,* known to the English-speaking world as the Jataka Tales, contains 547 stories in which, following upon a few words of wisdom, the Buddha explains an occurrence after his enlightenment in terms of something that happened in one of his former incarnations. The Chiang Mai priests, in an effort to strengthen the Buddhist tradition at home, seem to have translated folk tales into Pali and put them in the form of the *Nipāta Jātaka.*[5]

Although the Chiang Mai priests might have taken their material from written sources already part of the great tradition, a story of a golden prince, or a prince born in a golden shell, does not appear in the canonical *jātaka* collection in the southern Indian (Pali) tradition[6] or in the two most likely collections in the northern (Sanskrit) tradition.[7] Thus the story of Sang Thong may have been alive in Thailand as part of the oral tradition before it was written by the Chiang Mai priests as a story from a former life of the Buddha.

Phya Anuman Rajadhon, scholar of Thai culture and literature, feels that at least parts of the folk tale may have come from Tibet by way of the Shans, a Thai-speaking people living between the Chiang Mai and Burmese kingdoms, in what is now northeastern Burma. Dhanit Yupho, former director-general of the Thai Fine Arts Department, has written that an old Shan story (translated into English under the title "The Silver Oyster") may have contained details which contributed to the birth-story version of the Sang Thong legend.[8]

The possibility that the motif of a beautiful boy emerging from a conch shell came from Tibet (perhaps by way of the Shans) to Thailand seems heightened by the existence in Tibet of a cosmogonic myth including such a motif. This myth is the beginning of the genealogy of a great family of eastern Tibet, the Rlangs. Although the earliest citation we have of this genealogy is that of the fifth Dalai-Lama (A.D. 1617–82) in his Chronicle, the genealogy and the conch motif are most likely much earlier than this reference.[9] The genealogy of the Rlangs begins:

> From the essence of the five primordial elements a great egg came forth . . . Eighteen eggs came forth from the yolk of that great egg. The egg in the middle of the eighteen eggs, a conch egg, separated from the others. From this conch egg limbs grew, and then the five senses, all perfect, and it became a boy of such extraordinary beauty that he seemed the fulfillment of every wish.[10]

As early as the 8th or 9th century, Tibetan bards sang of the emergence of a hero from an egg.[11]

In Bengal, which has long had trade and religious connections with Tibet, Bengali women worshiping Vishnu tell a tale which is a close analogue to the first episode of *Sang Thong*.[12] A son "of surpassing beauty" emerges from the conch shell in which he was born. His mother breaks the shell to prevent his return to it.

One more folk tale, from Ceylon, mentions the birth of a prince in a *chank* (conch) shell.[13]

Combining of Motifs: Thai Creativity

Although the "child born in a conch shell" motif may thus have existed in the oral tradition of India, Ceylon, or Tibet before it was known in Thailand, the combination of this with other motifs of the episodic story may well have been a result of Thai creativity. After making a detailed study of the Thai translation of "Suvarna-Sankha-Jātaka" and comparing it with mural paintings of the Sang Thong story in a Buddhist temple in Uttaradit, a very old city between Bangkok and Chiang Mai, art historian Victor Kennedy feels that the spirit behind the combined motifs of the original Sang Thong story is the willfulness of a boy, and that *Sang Thong,* in a version untouched by priestly or princely interpolations, might well have begun in the Thai countryside.[14]

In the province of Uttaradit, where some people believe the Sang Thong story to be true, they call the ruins of a laterite enclosure the resting place of Prince Sang when disguised as a Negrito, or the polo ground where he entered the lists against Indra. Tung-yang, an old township in Uttaradit, claims to have been the city of Samon. In the province of Nakhon Sawan, close to Uttaradit Province, villagers identify a hill with the one where the ogress Phanthurat caught up with Prince Sang. The place in the stream where he magically called fishes

to him is, they say, beside a rock with odd formula-like
scratchings.[15] People in other parts of Thailand also claim
that Prince Sang's exploits occurred in or near a certain
township, body of water, or promontory, though more
of these claims seem to be made for the areas of Uttaradit and Nakhon Sawan than for other parts of Thailand. Thus, despite the uncertainty of scholars about
the origin of the Sang Thong story, many country Thais
feel the events of the tale actually happened in their own
surroundings.

The Oral Tradition: "Sang Thong" and "Lakhon Nok"

During the centuries between the writing of "Suvarna-
Sankha-Jātaka" and the dance-drama version of Rama
II, the Sang Thong legend was a lively part of the "little"
tradition of the country people. Either preserved directly
from an earlier oral tradition, or translated into Thai and
changed considerably from the Buddhist context of
"Suvarna-Sankha-Jātaka," the Sang Thong legend was
part of the type of folk drama later to be known as
lakhon nok (*nok:* "outside") to distinguish it from drama
originating in the court, known as *lakhon nai* (*nai:*
"inside"). My own experience of seeing village people
spontaneously begin to act out a story they are telling in-
clines me to think that the story may sometimes have
taken dramatic form as a group of people were being
amused by a storyteller.

The 17th-century account of *lakhon nok* quoted below

(my translation) is by Simon de La Loubère, envoy of Louis XIV to the Thai king Phra Narai, who reigned at Ayutthaya A.D. 1657–88:

> The presentation which is called "lacone" is a poem combining the epic and the dramatic, which goes on for three days, from eight in the morning to seven at night. These are serious stories in verse, sung by the actors who are always present [on stage] and who sing each in his turn. One of them sings the role of the story teller and the others that of the people speaking in the story; they are all men who sing and no women.[16]

René Nicholas, a French authority on the development of classical Siamese theater, feels that La Loubère was describing *lakhon nok,* because only men acted in the country and only women at court until the middle of the 19th century, when King Mongkut gave permission for women to act outside the court.[17]

Although the performance described by La Loubère was "serious," *lakhon nok* as described by later Thai and European writers was a form of drama in which actors often appealed to their audience with bawdy humor and satire. Actors sang their parts according to the general details of the story, in addition to providing humor familiar to the local audience. They sang in verses, fitting their words to dance motions which were faster and less graceful than those of court dancers.[18]

Court Drama: The Revival of "Sang Thong"

The Sang Thong legend moved fully into the "great" tradition again in the reign of Rama II (A.D. 1809–24), when the king and his court poets rewrote it as a dance-drama in verse form.

The final part of a written version of the Sang Thong legend had been preserved since the late 18th century, before the sack of the former capital at Ayutthaya.[19] A similarity of episodes and a very few similar lines lead one to believe that this version influenced at least part of the Rama II dance-drama. The very existence of this fragment may have contributed to the desire of Rama II to recreate *Sang Thong,* since he probably wanted to preserve or reestablish a cultural heritage from the few remains of the Thai literary tradition.

Although there exists no dramatic version of the first act of *Sang Thong* other than that included with the Rama II *lakhon,* Prince Damrong believed that it had also been written somewhat earlier than the reign of Rama II.[20] The choice of wording in Act One seems to show somewhat more concern for rhyme and less for meaning than that in the later acts. This act, upon which my close translation focuses, would, however, have had to be acceptable to the artist-king. A reconstruction of his purpose and method in composing the dance-drama is of interest, therefore, in accounting for the stylistic qualities of this first act and as an illustration of the interaction between "great" and "little" traditions.

Early in the reign of Rama II, according to Prince Damrong's history of this reign, the dancing girls in the king's court had reached a high level of performance. Thus the king must have wished to add new plays to their traditional repertoire, known collectively as *lakhon nai,* consisting of three plays: *Ramakian, Inao,* and *Unrut.*[21] We can, of course, only suggest how Rama II and his poets may have put *Sang Thong,* as well as at least five other plays from the rustic *lakhon nok* tradition, into verses furnishing words for his chorus and rhythm for his dancers. But the early life of Rama II, as well as Prince Damrong's reconstruction of the way courtly dance-dramas were composed and tested, does explain a style in which humorous, bawdy, "rural" sentiments came to be expressed in flowing, graceful lines.

Since the king had been brought up as a commoner in the countryside before his warrior father became king, he was quite likely acquainted with rural life as well as court life, and could still remember the ribald humor of *lakhon nok* as it was played for the pleasure of the people and of the spirits they wished to please. He and his poets, then, who included the famous Sunthon Phu and Rama II's eldest son, Prince Chesda, must have transformed this ribaldry into witticism acceptable to the higher classes, and then brought in the dancers to try their steps with the poetry. The poetry could then have been altered if the steps could not be fitted to it.[22]

Although the plot of "Suvarna-Sankha-Jātaka," the early prose story by the Chiang Mai priests, is very similar

to the plot of the poetic dance-drama of *Sang Thong,*
close comparison of the two reveals striking general
differences, as well as considerable difference in details.
The notion of Prince Sang as an incarnation of the
Buddha, so basic to the priest's story, is not apparent in
the king's version. On the other hand, the concept of
kingly responsibility, which was not in the priests' version, did enter King Rama's dance-drama. The workings
of karma, only implicit in the priests' story, are described and wondered about in the king's version. Animistic beliefs in spirits of trees, houses, and fields are not
part of the priests' story, though they are recurrent in
the king's version. The priests' story is humorless and
comparatively devoid of pathos, while both these qualities are very strong in the Rama II version of the story. I
am inclined to think that at least some of these differences
are attributable to a "little" tradition, which, as it developed in Thailand, had been elaborating themes reflecting
the feelings and everyday life of country people as they
told, read aloud, or acted the story.

STYLE: PERFORMANCE OF THE DANCE-DRAMA

Staging

In Thai drama, the elements of dance, music, and narration were never separated, as they were in the West,
leaving only a spoken script. For *Sang Thong,* this in-
tegration of dance, music, and narration has held true for

both city and country productions. Thus, although the verses appearing in the translation of "The Birth of Prince Sang" are dramatic literature, they do not appear in our Western form, as a script, but rather as a combination of narration, dialogue, and directions for music. The motions of the actors in Thai *lakhon* have been likened to the language of the dance. These motions are frequently not those a Westerner would expect as portrayals of a given feeling, but are composed of one or a combination of several stylized motions, sometimes involving only the hands, but more likely the whole body moving rhythmically to instrumental music or to the sung narration of the story.

Through the years *lakhon nok* and *lakhon nai* have borrowed each other's technical features to some extent. In both the recent National Theater production and a demonstration by an old country-woman of the way she danced the part of Prince Sang thirty years ago, the motions were meaningfully graceful. (Since the late 19th century, when Rama IV lifted the ban on women appearing in *lakhon* outside the court, a woman has frequently played the role of Prince Sang, for traditionally a Thai hero has been a graceful figure.) However, in both city and country the actions of the comic characters have always been quick and unrestrained.

For National Theater productions, dancers must learn the centuries-old movements expressive of feelings; however, if a dancer is particularly admired, the slight variations with which he interprets a part may be passed on to later dancers of the role. Before the days of the National Theater, when Thailand was still an absolute monarchy, a Negrito called Kenang was featured in *Sang Thong* when the play was presented for the court of King Chulalongkorn (Rama V). The king had taken the Negrito into his household as an orphan child some years before. Kenang created something of a sensation in the role by playing the part without the usual mask for the acts in which Prince Sang wears the disguise of a Negrito.[23]

The extent to which the text was narrated by a person offstage or was sung by the players themselves seems to have varied in different places and at different times. La Loubère's account of *lakhon nok* at the end of the 17th century includes both a narrator and singers of parts. The style of the Rama II version indicates that, as this version was originally written, a narrator sang much of the story while dancers "spoke the language of the dance," with some ad-libbing between verses. Each verse, as indicated in the translation of Act One, usually focuses on one figure. Country people tell me that the last time *Sang Thong* was given in their village, each dancer sang his own part, describing both the situation and his feelings as he danced.

In the 1968 National Theater production of two of the later acts of *Sang Thong,* the main narration was sung in long verses, by a single voice alternating with a chorus line by line. In short verses there was only the single voice. The narrators sat with the percussion orchestra, just offstage. With them sat a man specially skilled in reading the lines quickly, so that the narrators could hear and repeat them. Unlike the Western prompter, the *khon bawk bot* was constantly active. The narrators, however, did not simply repeat what he said, but put the words to an elaborated melody and rhythm which would in turn fit with the dance. The dancers spoke their own words. (These are indicated by quotation marks in the translation of Act One, which follows.)

As Dhanit Yupho has observed, the chorus developed in connection with costuming. Thai court dancers for centuries used elaborate costumes with many traditional pieces. These costumes were so intricate that special people were needed to dress the dancers, who were, then as now, sewn into their costumes. After the costumers had performed their duties there was nothing for them to do, so they were utilized as a chorus to alternate in the narration with the primary singer. When he became director-general of the Fine Arts Department twenty years ago, Dhanit Yupho urged dancers to help dress each other as an economy measure. The tradition of the chorus, however, remained.[24]

As the translation of "The Birth of Prince Sang" indicates, specialized music is played between many of the verses by an ensemble consisting, in its simplest form, of a xylophone-like instrument with wooden strips, two types of drums, a reed pipe, and a small pair of cymbals. Occasionally a melody is played on one or more string instruments. This music, each rhythm of which is significantly familiar to a Thai audience, can indicate changes of scene, making scenery unnecessary. Narration and music suffice to indicate changes of time and place to the audience.

According to the emotion to be expressed, a single instrument performs, or several are played in unison. There is thus specialized music to follow the actions of a person of high status, to indicate that people of low status are leaving the scene, to express sadness, to indicate an important happening (often one which involves magic), to follow a person of high rank in the city or country, or to express the soft, sweet feelings of a love scene. Occasionally the music may accompany the speaking player, as in a love scene, but more frequently it is interspersed between verses.

Reading

Some time ago I came across a young Thai woman reading *Sang Thong* in a lovely singing voice. No one else was in the room. Her reading was in the *thamnawng* style, which children learn early in their school years as they begin to study poetry, giving distinctive rhythm and melody to different types of Thai poetry. Shyly the young Thai woman, who had been brought up in the countryside, ventured that she had been considered a good reader when she was a child. Having spent many hours watching *lakhon,* she had acquired its *thamnawng* style.

Rama II and his poets wrote *Sang Thong* to be sung aloud. They used a form called *klon bot lakhon*, in which the syllables in a line vary between six and nine. In recent years, *klon bot lakhon,* like other forms of poetry, has been written in two double columns. Thus what Westerners would consider a "line" begins in the left column; the next line begins on the same level in the right column. The *klon bot lakhon* form uses rhymes, sometimes occurring between ends of lines, but more frequently between the end of a line in one column and the middle of a line in the other column.

Alliteration and assonance, valued in Thai daily speech, are used often in *klon bot lakhon,* as in other forms of poetry in Thailand.

THE LIVING TRADITION IN THAILAND

Although "The Birth of Prince Sang," the first act of *The Golden Prince of the Conch Shell,* is no longer presented on stages in Thailand, other episodes of *Sang Thong* are currently produced at the National Theater, satirized by university students, and played zestfully— following the story, if not the text—at the shrine of Bangkok's guardian spirit and at town temple-fairs. All nine episodes have recently been published as a "cremation volume" honoring a respected official. City and village children become acquainted with the first act early in their schooling and with other acts in later years, as they continue their studies.

The National Theater

   Sang Thong as part of the "great" tradition might have been lost when the end of the absolute monarchy in Thailand (1932) made extensive royal patronage of dancers and musicians no longer possible. However, with slow, painful efforts the National Theater was formed. So popular has *Sang Thong* been that in 1954 a version combining two episodes, "The Marriage of the King's Daughters" (Acts Five and Six) and "Hunting and Fishing" (Act Seven), ran through 127 performances. In 1960 one of the later acts of *Sang Thong*, "The Polo Match," was given. All of these productions used very elaborate scenery, unlike the *lakhon nok* staging by the country folk or by the court of Rama II.

   Honoring the 200th anniversary (1968) of the birth of Rama II, "The Marriage of the King's Daughters" and "Hunting and Fishing" were presented in the open-air theater surrounded by the brilliantly colored roofs of the National Museum. Young and old crowded to the simple stage, children so close that they could almost touch the actors and actresses. No scenery or props were used except the traditional couch for Thai dance-drama. The narrator, chorus, actors, and actresses followed exactly the Rama II text.

University Satire

   Also honoring the anniversary of Rama II, Thammasat University students presented a version of *Sang Thong,* "The Mother-in-Law," based on the episode in which Queen Montha tries to persuade Prince Sang (disguised as a Negrito) to compete with Indra. Written by the rapier-like pen of author and journalist M. R. Kukrit Pramoj, "The Mother-in-Law" was acted with cutting satire on current figures, which M. R. Kukrit feels was part of the earliest *lakhon nok* style of the country people.

Shrine Offerings

Hidden behind encroaching modern buildings in the heart of Bangkok is a small shrine to its guardian spirit, the *chao phaw lak mueang.* Since widely known plays as well as new ones are given here continually, an episode from *Sang Thong* is frequently presented.

On weekends the little enclosure around the pole representing the spirit is so crowded that one can hardly move toward the tables covered with eggs, meat, steamed rice cakes, and other foods, or toward the stage where gaily dressed men and women dance, sing, and speak in the *likay* style. Performers of *likay,* a popular dramatic form developed in the 20th century, use some of the *lakhon* dance motions, but less artfully than do performers of *lakhon nok* or *lakhon nai.* Originally *likay* performers were often taught by court dancers, but this is no longer true. The *likay* style is freer than that of either *lakhon nok* or *lakhon nai,* and permits more ad-libbing; there is more speaking and less singing, fewer musical instruments are used (the musicians are limited to percussion instruments only), and certain sounds and intonations distinguish *likay* diction. Since common people find *likay* great fun, they feel it is an appropriate style in which to play an episode of the Sang Thong story for the spirit they wish to please.

According to the classical dancer Malulee Pinsuvana, a poor woman with some dramatic skill might go to a person who wants to repay the spirit for his good fortune. When she asks if she can play some part in return for a small amount of money, he may ask if she can play one of the characters in the story of Sang Thong. Invariably the answer will be, "I can." The date will be set; with little practice of dance steps or lines, she will play, not according to any text but from memory of the story, using some of the lines she may have heard from the Rama II version.

Although educated Thais say there is no art in *likay* at the shrine, their children, as well as those of common people, can be overheard urging their nurses or their parents to let them stay to the end of a performance. And so the story, though it may be presented gracelessly, becomes part of the children's lives.

Rural Performances

Ten or twenty years ago the playing of *Sang Thong* by a group of traveling performers, in either *lakhon nok* or *likay* style, was a common occurrence in towns and rice villages. Now it seems to be far rarer. But performances much like those at the shrine of the guardian spirit in Bangkok are still given at temple fairs in Nakhon Pathom, a provincial town.

Villagers in Sagatiam, west of Bangkok, tell of performances of *Sang Thong* given until about ten years ago. The head-teacher of the school taught village people the parts, and they performed in the surrounding area for various festivals or for people wishing to make repayment to the spirits for some good fortune. It is difficult to ascertain the extent to which such players followed a text or merely followed the general lines of the story, making up their words and inventing their dance movements as they went along. Today, the eyes of old and middle-aged villagers glisten as they talk of performances of *Sang Thong*. Mrs. Bunsong Jai-ngam, for example, daughter of a woman who often acted with the head-teacher's group, had been talking to us of past performances as she squatted on the floor washing dishes. Suddenly she put down her dishcloth, stood up, and began to dance. The words she sang, as she recalled the old performance, were exactly those of Rama II's version. The part she spontaneously danced and sang was from Act Two, in which the little Prince Sang, eager to see the toy promised by a soldier sent to kill him, stretches out his hand and is caught. Since other village people have spontaneously related poignant portions of the drama, I am inclined to think that these especially were carried, word for word, from the "great" tradition of the courtly version to the "little" tradition of country people.

Memorial Volumes

At the cremation ceremony of a respected Thai, the family presents guests with a volume, sometimes having special meaning to the deceased or one of his relatives, sometimes chosen by the National Library as having general worth. In 1961 a special printing of the Rama II version of *Sang Thong* was done for the cremation of Police Lieutenant-Colonel Kowit Praphrupan. In answer to my letter asking why *Sang Thong* had been chosen, his older brother responded, with elegant simplicity, "It is a treasure of the Thai people."

School Programs

A piece of literature, particularly a long one, is seldom taught all at one time in Thai schools. Instead, an episode appropriate to the students' understanding is given them to read. Although many Thai students go far enough to study "The Choice of Husbands," "The Winning of Rochana," and "Hunting and Fishing," which are considered finer Thai poetry, fourth-graders already know the play from their study of "The Birth of Prince Sang."

Jaroen Jai-ngam, a Thai village teacher, explains that

when "The Birth of Prince Sang" was taught twenty years ago, the only purpose was memorization of portions of the text by the school children. Today, the teacher reads the poetry to the children in the *thamnawng* style, which is quite different from the way Western poetry is read. The students repeat after him, to get a feeling for the sounds. The teacher then tells the story, explaining names and trying to interest his students in the characters. (Mr. Jaroen confides that he himself likes *Sang Thong* better than the greater classic *Ramakian,* because the characters in *Sang Thong* seem to have more human feelings.) The children read the first part of "The Birth of Prince Sang," which has been put into simple prose. Then they read the few verses of poetry which tell of the son's feeling that it is his responsibility to help his mother in return for her care, and the teacher tries to help them feel the importance of this parent–child relationship.

Mrs. Malulee Pinsuvana, who has danced several parts in *Sang Thong* in the classical theater, recalls that when she was a small child and had to choose a new notebook for school, she would repeatedly buy one that had scenes from "The Birth of Prince Sang" on the cover. It is now the favorite story of her own small sons.

SANG THONG
IN OTHER SOUTHEAST ASIAN COUNTRIES

The Chiang Mai priests wrote the *Pannāsa Jātaka* on palm leaves in fifty bundles, according to Prince Damrong, who also noted that copies of the *Pannāsa Jātaka* still existed in 20th-century Luang Prabang, Laos, and Phnom Penh, Cambodia. Quite possibly copies of the Chiang Mai palm-leaf manuscripts were sent to Laos, Cambodia, and Burma, with which Chiang Mai priests had contact.

Laos

At the present time a Pali palm-leaf manuscript of the Sang Thong story, generally similar to "Suvarna-Sankha-Jātaka," exists in a Buddhist temple, Wat Ong Tue, in Vientiane. Other such manuscripts existed in the past, according to Maha Kikeo Oudom of the Library of Fine Arts in Vientiane, but were lost during the Siamese occupation of Laos in the 19th century.

In another story which is very popular in Laos, the hero, Sin Xay, has a brother called Thao Sang who, though born in a shell, has few other similarities to the Thai Prince Sang. As in the Thai version of the Sang Thong story, the queen, mother of Sin Xay and Thao Sang, is sent weeping from the kingdom because of the unnatural birth.

In northeastern Thailand, which has alternately been Laotian and Thai territory, stories about both Sin Xay and Sang Thong have been popular through the years. Between the time of a death and a cremation, when friends of the deceased stay to keep the family company, a villager will often read one of the stories from a palm-leaf manuscript. Professor Visudh Busyakul is presently translating one of these manuscripts, written in old Laotian script, in which the Sang Thong story is quite different in detail from either the "Suvarna-Sankha-Jātaka" or the Rama II *Sang Thong*. In this Laotian version the king and queen are even pleased with the birth of a son in a shell!

Cambodia

A Cambodian classical dance-drama known as *Preas Sang* follows the episodes of the Thai version from the point where Rochana chooses Prince Sang, disguised as an ugly Negrito, as her husband, to the point where the king of Samon honors his formerly despised son-in-law after the latter has engaged in combat with Indra.[25]

This Cambodian version does not, however, contain the birth of Prince Sang, the treachery of his father's jealous minor wife, the prince's descent to the world of the serpents, his nurture by the ogress Phanthurat, or King Yosawimon's search for his son. Thus the *Preas Sang* episodes performed in Cambodia are the same ones from *Sang Thong* currently performed by the National Theater of Thailand. In both countries other acts present in the Rama II version of *Sang Thong* are omitted in current performances. Possibly this similarity of staged episodes results from the influence of Thai dancers who went to Cambodia in the 18th and 19th centuries and revived the art of Cambodian classical dancing. This art had died in Cambodia when the Thais defeated Ang-kor (1431) and brought the Cambodian palace dancers to the Thai capital. James Brandon writes that "the Royal Cambodian Ballet of today is actually a reimporta-tion of ancient Khmer dance, as modified by some twenty generations of Thai court artists."[26] Since Rama II's version had been written by the 19th century, and since certain acts may have been performed more often than others, it is conceivable that those acts preferred in Thai-land were taken to Cambodia by Thai dancers.

Burma

In Burma there seems to be little, if any, acquaintance with the Sang Thong story today. Thai scholars be-lieve that manuscripts of the *Pannāsa Jātaka* sent from Chiang Mai to Burma were burned by a king who felt they were not true birth-stories.[27] Although a Pali ver-sion of *Pannāsa Jātaka* was published in Rangoon in 1911, the "Suvarna-Sankha-Jātaka" was not part of it.[28]

Thus the presence of the Sang Thong story in some, although not all, of Southeast Asia reflects cultural dif-ferences and similarities in that area of the world.

THAI VIEWS OF LIFE IN THEIR ASIAN CONTEXT

The anthropologist Margaret Mead conceives of "cultural character" as arising out of "a circular system [in] which . . . the method of child rearing, the presence of a particular literary tradition, the nature of the domestic and public architecture, the religious beliefs, the political system, are all conditions within which a given kind of personality develops."[29]

*Sang Thong'*s long period of development in Thailand, the views expressed in it, and the keen interest felt in its story by many present-day Thais place it in the literary tradition which is an integral part of the "circle" forming Thai cultural character. This drama, moreover, reflects most of the other elements mentioned by Margaret Mead in the passage quoted above.

In "The Birth of Prince Sang," as well as in later episodes of *Sang Thong,* views are expressed concerning the responsibility of kingship and the respect due to it, the mutually helpful relationship that should exist between a parent and child, the effects of deeds of one's past life upon one's present life, the pragmatic and manipulative use of both natural and supernatural means to achieve desired results, and the importance of status relationships. Most of these values and views of the world are expressed in some detail, as are the depictions of the particular reciprocal relationship the king has with the queen and both have with their people, the particular kinds of spirits that are thought to exist, and the ways a person tries to influence the workings of karma.

Few, if any, of the traditional views of life found in *Sang Thong* are distinctively Thai in the sense that individual elements cannot be found elsewhere in the world, particularly in Asia; but in their totality they form a distinctively Thai configuration. As the notes to Acts One through Nine will point out, the themes in *Sang Thong,* as portrayed through the dramatic events and in the attitudes of its human and mythological characters, reveal a common Hindu–Buddhist–Brahman cultural and literary heritage as well as a peculiarly Thai development in which foreign features were adapted and assimilated according to Thai values and understandings. Furthermore, Thais of diverse ranks adapted such foreign features to their own ways of life. *Sang Thong* in its present literary form, and as translated and summarized in this volume, comes from two divergent streams: the long process of oral transmission existing mainly among the folk, and the more sophisticated written tradition perpetuated by temple scribes and court poets. These streams inevitably continue to diverge in present-day Thailand, and both traditions carry indelible traces of Rama II's ingenious 19th-century fusion of rustic and courtly drama.

Sang Thong

THE GOLDEN PRINCE
OF THE CONCH SHELL

List of Characters
(in order of appearance)

ACT ONE

KING YOSAWIMON, father of Prince Sang

QUEEN CHANTHEWI, wife of King Yosawimon, mother of Prince Sang

QUEEN CHANTHA, minor wife of King Yosawimon

MAID of Queen Chantha

ASTROLOGER, prophet of doom for Yosawimon's kingdom

OLD MAN AND WOMAN, peasants protecting Queen Chanthewi

PRINCE SANG (Sang Thong), child born in a conch shell; hero of later episodes

❦ ACT ONE

The Birth of Prince Sang

Now I'd like to tell the story[1]
of King Yosawimon[2] the great ruler.
He had no son, and thus his royal line would end.
One day, during his inspection of the city,[3]
the people cried out that he must have a son.
The Bearer of the Land[4] felt aflame, as if pierced by arrows.
He could not eat, nor could he take a bath.[5]
Sitting, sleeping, he felt great anguish.
The people were desperate; they saw no sign of hope.
The more they thought, the more restless they became.
They pitied the king who had treasure
but no son of great dignity.
So the king spoke with his queen,
explaining all in great detail:
"Come, my Heart,[6] help me[7] think this over.
Let's search and find our own merit.[8]
Let's pay homage to all the divinities.[9]
Let's keep the precepts[10] to strengthen our deeds.
Tell each lady in the inner court[11] to make all these efforts.
Perhaps the reward will come to those who've built up merit."

47

Then[12]
the queen felt no jealousy.
She greeted the king and received his orders.
She said, "Do not be anxious, or feel unhappy about me.
I shall depend upon you and give my life to you.[13]
I shall never raise objections to your wishes.
It will be according to any wife's merit.
So put aside your worries."

Listening to the queen,
he was pleased by her response.
He ordered wise old women[14]
to prepare a worshipful offering.[15]
At dusk, when the sun had gone down,
they made preparations in the palace.
They told the maids
What each one was to do
to arrange the offering
of incense sticks and different kinds of candles.
"Every day, each take a turn
to sleep here, beside me, all of you."[16]

(Maids and minor wives ad-lib between verses.)

Then
the king was fully determined.
He saw the women lying beside each other
and spoke to them of the heart of the matter:
"Now look here, all you women,

we have a purpose and have decided
to have a son.
I care not[17] whose child it may be.
I urge all to pray[18] for a son
to whatever powers you wish.
Whoever bears a son:
the kingdom I'll give to her child."
Speaking as he went to his offering table,
he urged his honored queen
to pay homage[19] to the deities
in the golden room of his palace.

(Music indicates a person of high status has been acting. For the following verse the narrator and chorus use a melody indicating a ceremony is being performed.)

Lighting incense sticks and candles,
so that there was beauty shining everywhere,
both the king and his queen set their hearts
on their one pure desire.
Bowing respectfully, they prayed together:
"In the name of the royal power,[20]
we two have governed the people and priests[21]
with goodness and justice for a long time.
We have no beloved son
to give happiness to the people in the future.[22]
Lord of the Land,[23] most powerful, be kind;
please grant us the birth of a child."
Having done this, the king slept.

Each day, missing none, he kept the five precepts.
And held the ten virtues:[24] he did no injustice to anyone.
He went to the sleeping place quickly.

Now I'll tell the story
of a divinity in heaven.
When he was to end his heavenly existence,
his strange discomforts were many.
His shining halo dimmed.
All his possessions seemed worn.
The deity was startled and aghast.
He knew in his heart he would die.
Then, as he mused and looked down on the world,
the reason became clear to him.
The king named Yosawimon
was presenting offerings and petitioning the deities.
"Other divinities will come and urge me
to leave the heaven called Dawadueng.
I'll not wait; I'll be reborn at once.
I'll not let them come to tell me.
I'll go down to be born as a man,
leading a pious life on earth."
Thinking this, he held his breath till his heavenly existence
    was ended
and his spirit entered the womb of the queen.[25]

(Music indicates slight sadness.
The narrator and chorus sing the following verse to an espe-
cially slow melody.)

Then
King Yosawimon dreamed about
the day when he would have a son.
The dream entered his sleep at night.
It was seen to be a divine omen.[26]
The sun burst forth with color.
He was startled to consciousness,
remembering all the dream's details.

At dawn the sun shone brightly.
He bathed and attired himself handsomely.
Then he went to the audience hall,
and sat on a throne supported by sculptures of gold.

(Music indicates a person of high status is acting.)

All the soldiers and attendants went to the king
to receive his command.
He said to the astrologer, great as one could desire:
"Look into my dream.
I dreamed that the sun, a being of great power,
fell in front of my face and to the right.
A little star also lay in the earth:
I turned to grasp it.
In my left hand was a star;
in my right was the sun.
Only the sun disappeared.
When I cried and cried I got it back.
About three o'clock, before dawn,

I reached out again and was startled from sleep.
Predict good or evil to follow, do not conceal it.[27]
Astrologer, speak!"

At that time,
the astrologer had no equal.
His calculations were made and it was clear in his mind:
The king would have a son.
Therefore he said: "According to the dream, I predict:
The queen at the right[28]
will become pregnant with a son
who will have much merit.
He will be parted from the court
though later will return to the kingdom.
The star means a daughter
will be born to a suitable wife.
Crying in the king's dream indicates
One day he will admire his son, happy and laughing.
The prediction follows the dream to the end.
Let the king hear these details!"

(Courtiers ad-lib between verses.)

Hearing this,
the king, satisfied and happy,
graciously spoke to the astrologer:
"If it is as you say I shall reward you.
The people complained that there must be a son.
I am so desperate, for I must do something.

I am ashamed, more ashamed than anyone else."
So saying, he went into the women's court.

(Music indicates a person of high status is acting.)

He went to inform his wife,
to tell her all the details.
The king gradually had a feeling of well-being.
Chanthewi[29] became more beautiful night and day.
Bright gold her skin;
her breasts darkened;
her blood vessels stood out,
indicating her pregnancy.
Her skin became creamy, her face brightened.
The king loved her very much.
He chose many young girls with beautiful figures
to surround the fair lady.[30]
Then he teasingly asked: "How are the rest of you?
Are you pregnant yet?" he chuckled.
"Take the trouble to put creamy powder on your skins!"
Laughingly, he entertained himself.

(King and women ad-lib.)

Then seeing Chantha, a minor wife,
her breasts quickly becoming firm, he wondered.
Surely it meant she too was pregnant.
The king gave her many things.
The other wives, who were not pregnant,

interpreted the dream, saw the treasures, and were
  unhappy.
They bowed and left the presence of the Bearer of the
  Discus.[31]
Chantha too retired to her room.

*(Musicians play a melody indicating that people below the
level of the king, but not commoners, have acted.)*

When Chantha reached her room,
thinking sadly and jealously,
she was overwhelmed with desire for the throne.
The king had said whoever was pregnant
would receive treasure that would give the child the
  right to rule.
If there were two, he would think of another way.
But the king and queen, having the same position, would
  love each other.
So the second child would be unhappy.
How could he be the successor to the throne?
The maids would laugh together.
The more she thought about it, the more depressed she
  became.
So she called her cook to the room:
"Good maid, you must pity me:
Money, rice, gold, and silver will be given.
Help by keeping your lips sealed.
Take the gold and give it to the astrologer.
I have written a secret letter with an order.

I hope I can trust you completely."
She took off her ring and gave it to the maid with no
    hesitancy:
"I am satisfied with you and for the moment have this
    for you."

At once
the maid took the bribe.
She paid respect, bowing low, and said:
"Your daughter[32] will not betray you.
I would die with my royal mother.
I will never depend on another.
If Mother succeeds, I shall be happy."
She took the package of gold and put on the ring.

(Rapid music indicates a person of low status has been acting.)

Arriving at the house of the old astrologer,
she went straight up on the porch.[33]
Having greeted[34] him, she gave him the gold from
    Chantha:
"Royal mother sent this from the women's court,
Saying Grandfather[35] is kind.
She asks you to fulfill her wishes
So that friendship may remain."
Then she quickly handed him the letter.

Then
the chief astrologer wondered greatly.

He took the letter,
put on his glasses, looked, then knew the heart of the text.
He thought secretly in his heart,
greedily and without fear:
"If I don't reverse my prophecy,
these three *chang*[36] of gold must be returned.
If I do solve Chantha's problem,
five *chang* will be mine."
So he spoke to the maid with delight:
"It will be nothing to solve the problem."
Turning to see that no one was in the house,
hesitating, but wanting to make love, he said:
"Maid, go into the bedroom:
please pick up the cigarettes near my bed."

(Astrologer and maid ad-lib.)

The maid was embarrassed, for she knew his thoughts:
"Oh, Grandfather, how can you speak like this?
Who could go to your bed?
You have so many things that could be stolen."
She swatted his hand away and bid farewell,
"Don't, I want nothing to do with you."
She rushed away immediately
to the palace to tell what had happened.

(fast music)

Meanwhile

the lovely head of the forbidden women
took care of herself.
Her pregnancy developed beautifully for ten months.[37]
At almost the auspicious time,
her stomach, both large and small parts, descended.[38]
A desire to push forth the child, then her pulsing heart,
   were warnings.
The child slid down a little farther.
Pain spread through her body,
as though her life would break in pieces.
She called the women who cared for her.
They came together and stood around her.
She called and moaned:
"Help, hurry, hurry, maids!"
Her body trembled, tensed, pushed, held, then relaxed.
The queen cried out, but with no strength remaining.

Then
the women, who looked after the queen skillfully,
turning the stomach and touching it, wondered.
They found it hard, with no struggle within,
but round and rolling: they wondered.
Astonished, they found nowhere the body they sought.
Some went to the king
to let him know what was happening.

(Fast music indicates women are hurrying away. This is different from the music played when the maid hurried to or from the astrologer's house.)

When they greeted the king,
they said the queen at the right
would give birth to a royal son.
"Please come, Ruler of the Sky."

Then
King Yosawimon hastened, feeling delighted.
"I will see my dear little child
today, my beloved."
Hurrying, as one who yet has no son,
the king was infinitely happy.
The women of the inner court streamed after him:
Beautiful Chantha followed too.

(Fast music indicates people of high status are hurrying. This type of music would not be used for the usual slow movements of a king.)

The king said to please the queen:
"Don't be afraid.
Officials are making arrangements
and carrying out their duties
to prepare in all the land
announcements of the birth of our child."

Meanwhile
the queen's stomach became turbulent,
not yet light and free of pain.
The pain was like a rope pulling.

Deeds from her former life[39]
would keep her from the treasure.
There was the birth of a prince at the proper time
But the son was hidden in a conch shell.

*(Women ad-lib, accompanied by a stringed instrument playing
slowly and sweetly.)*

The queen, with beating heart, was frightened.
The maids in the room were startled too.
The king felt as if his eyes were bleeding.
A conch horn blew and drums beat.
Desolate, he heard the glorious sound.
He ordered the maids out of the room.
He felt he would die,
ashamed before them all.[40]
Then he spoke to the queen:
"Beloved wife, what can we think about this?
It should not be, but is.
When there is no child, there is no happiness.
We asked a favor of the deities:
The time came and this is the result.
I am ashamed before the people.
I would like to stop breathing, and in death escape from
    shame."

Listening to him speak,
the queen felt as though her head had been cut off, had
    fallen, and was rolling away.

She beat her breast with her hands,[41]
then bowed, raised her hands in respect, and cried:
"Oh, beloved husband,
what deeds I must have done!
I am sorry I carried and gave birth to this thing.
I was happy with the purpose of having the good name of
    your wife.
I had no idea it would bring such shame:
I have made you share the disgrace.
Take your sword and kill me.
It is better to die than to make you lose honor."

Then
Chantha had the chance she wanted.
She and the astrologer, confident of each other,
went to see the king.[42]
She said: "It is a pity
and I am amazed.
Your son, sadly, is a shell.
There has been nothing like this before.
I am pregnant too, so I fear for my own condition:
Will the outcome be good or bad, I wonder?
Originally the astrologer predicted
that when the queen became pregnant,
the son would have great merit.
He predicted this according to the dream.
Let your queen lie by the fire to cure her illness,[43]
then the Bearer of Truth should ask the astrologer all."

Hearing Chantha's words
that the result of past deeds would separate the couple,
whether a trick or not, the king did not know:
"It's true that the astrologer prophesied
that two would surely become pregnant.
Now it is true as he said.
He has always had respect and renown,
but a son has been born like this.
All right, I shall go to ask him,
to be certain of how matters are."
So he told the queen to rest by the fire,
and he left for the court immediately.

(Music indicates a person of high status is leaving.)

He sent someone to bring the astrologer to him.
The king asked about the last dreaming:
"Originally you prophesied the lady would become
   pregnant;
so it is, as the words spoken.
Why is the little child a conch shell?
You have erred or distorted the dream, for it is not as you
   said,
that there would be a son with merit.
Your words were false.
Make a new prophecy, speak truly.
I shall weep till my tears turn to blood.
Whatever sort of misfortune this is,
speak, astrologer, don't conceal it."

Then
the great astrologer, having accepted the bribe,
was sure his plan could drive the queen
far away from the palace.
He pretended to hunt in the text
and slowly changed his prophecy to the opposite of
    truth.
Then he told the king that
what he had prophesied was not untrue:
"The fortunes of the kingdom have changed.
What the king has said about a son
is the result of the past deeds of his wife.
If the son had been a human being,
he would have had honor and fame in the kingdom.
Now the fate is that misfortune will prevail until every-
    thing is gone.
The households of the kingdom will deteriorate to ruin.
Death and ruin.
If the king orders the queen to go far from the kingdom,
it will be calm and happy.
Don't hesitate and put it off a long time.
The fires of the god of death will burn the kingdom."[44]

As the king listened to the astrologer
it seemed his heart would stop and there would be no life
    in his body:
"Is it really true, astrologer,
that we who have always been together must now part?"
While feeling desolate and sighing,

he held back his tears and went away.
He entered the room walled with shimmering glass,
looking for his wife, the protectress of his spirit.[45]

(Music indicates a person of high status is leaving.)

Despairing, the king threw himself down
and spoke to her as he cried:
"Oh, the consequences of our past deeds
will make us go far from each other, my Eyes.
This should not be, but is.
We both suffer for the son we'd have loved.
The astrologer predicts much misfortune, my wife,
saying my Jewel is a bearer of evil.[46]
If you stay longer the people will be angry,
the kingdom will be ruined: so I must insist you go.
I too will be brokenhearted.
You have done not the slightest wrong.[47]
Feeling such pity and love,
Who could separate calmly?[48]
There is no reason for it to happen.[49]
We didn't know we'd have to part."

Having heard this,
and feeling like one who'd been killed,
frightened as one burned in fire at the end of the world,
with beating heart but with the spirit gone,[50]
she embraced the feet of her dear husband,
beat her breast and cried:

"I asked you to kill me
but you said you loved me and didn't want to do it.
Now the astrologer has changed the meaning of the
  dream.
You should consider again the details.
You are sending me away because you don't want to
  kill me,
but it is the same as death for us to part."
Crying, she strained to move her body
as though she were dying of sorrow.
She hid her face in her husband's lap,
so frightened, she fainted and could not speak.

(very sorrowful music with a crying sound)

"Oh, my dearest,
your body is as cold as one dead.
You cried but are now silent.
You lie on my lap without breathing."

(same sorrowful music)

"Oh, Chanthewi, my beloved,
lift your face, don't cry.
Your husband's heart is breaking.
Get up, and let us talk together.
I am speaking to you, why don't you answer?
My dearest is dying, so true.
You implored me to kill you.

What can we do?
Parting will be a great hardship
but if we don't die we'll see each other some day.
Why do you not lift your face and say farewell?
Dearest, don't make too much of this.[51]
If you die, only you can leave the trouble.
Leaving me in that way would make me desolate."
Crying while embracing her,
he too slipped from consciousness.

(same sorrowful music)

Then
Chantha was full of scheming ways.
Seeing two unconscious people lying one on the other,
from a vase she poured water of roses,
rubbing it over the bodies,
gradually bringing the two to consciousness.

Then
she comforted them with words from her hard heart:
"It's your fate from deeds of past lives; you can't
    blame anyone.
We've no reason to think the astrologer is wrong.
We've respected him for a long time.
You must go to end the fated trouble, Chanthewi.
If you do, the ill fate will diminish.
In this way you will not die.
This will not kill you.

When the ill fate has decreased,
then we will take you back."

Meanwhile
the king, gradually coming back to consciousness,
heard the words of Chantha
and thought about them sadly.
He did not suspect the words
because the turn of fate is that way.[52]
So he said:
"Chantha, help make preparations.
Give Chanthewi food,
money, silver, gold, and dried provisions."
He ordered the workers of the court to prepare
a beautiful curtained boat
to take her across the border
and to exile his dearest wife.
Crying as he spoke and looked at Chanthewi,
the king was ashamed,[53] and did not turn toward
    Chantha.

Then
Chantha, who felt very jealous,
was happy to hear the words. She took the order,
pretended to wipe away tears, and left the room.

(Music indicates a person of high status is leaving.)

Chantha prepared nothing,

nor gave silver, gold, rice, or fish.
She whispered orders to her maid, who thought as she:
"Take money to the king's men
and say 'Have pity and help us.
Take the queen away. Don't respect her position.[54]
Go far across the border of the country.
Then kill her,
or do as you like with her, but don't allow her to return
    to reign.'
Keep this secret as though there were nothing.
I will repay you and give you much more.
Do not speak about this or let anyone hear."

(Chantha and maid ad-lib.)

When this was finished Chantha returned to the king's
    palace,
saying she had done everything as he had ordered:
"Silver, gold, food of every kind
are ready with a boat to go along the river.
Now, the people[55] of the kingdom
are dissatisfied and desire to rebel.
They are meeting together in anger,
for they think the birth of the shell will bring trouble.
They are saying the queen leaves the court too slowly.
They will destroy the kingdom in their distress.
I'm afraid I shall have trouble too.
Everything will be disastrous because of the bad deeds,"

Hearing this news,

the king was anxious and fearful.

Believing in Chantha's words of what would happen
because of karma,

he thought that everything was true.

He looked for a long time upon the face of the queen.

Tears welled up in his eyes as he sighed deeply.

When he had to speak, he felt constrained,[56] unable to
think

because of his love for his wife.

If he did not make her go,

he feared the words Chantha had spoken.

Speaking diplomatically,[57] he said:

"My dearest, you're a person with deeds from a past life.

You separated animals who were meant to be in couples.[58]

It's now your turn to suffer misfortune.

If you have this karma to suffer and you don't go to pay
the consequences,[59]

the people will cause destruction.

It's not that I do not love you,[60]

and share your feelings," he cried.

"If you don't die, you will have the results of good deeds
too.[61]

When good fortune comes and the results of bad deeds
are finished, we'll see each other again."

While speaking, he could not look at his wife's face.

Tears flowing, he turned away

and walked into the room of sparkling glass.

Pulling the curtains of gold together, he cried.[62]

(Two musical themes combine, one for a person of high status leaving and another for great sorrow.)

Then
the queen beat her breast as she thought of her husband.
Feeling she would die,
crying till almost unconscious,
she thought she would implore him to delay,
but he had turned his face and gone from her.
Overwhelmed[63] by sorrow and anger, she cried and cried:
"Why do you[64] go away from me?
My old deeds force me to leave you.
I[65] shall not object.
But I ask the favor of delay to lie by the fire
just for seven days.[66]
When my body is again normal[67]
I shall wander and hide in the forest.
If you're not angry and don't want to punish me,
why not order that I stay for a time?"
While speaking she beat her breast,
hardly breathing, close to death, from crying for her
    husband.
Her maids could not hold back their tears
as they sat beside the golden bed.[68]

(sorrowful music)

At that time
Chantha's "goodness" was incomparable.[69]

Fulfilled in all her desires,
She turned her face and spoke further
to her maid, who shared her thoughts,
saying: "Listen to this order from the king.
Take the queen down
and deliver her to the soldiers.
If you are slow, the people will be very angry
and will usurp the power of the throne.
Because of Chanthewi's deeds,
if you are late, the kingdom will be in danger."

At once
the maid, a woman of the same heart,
who knew the trick,
secretly went to the queen.
She said the Ruler of the Land[70]
had declared he was very worried
and afraid his enemies would strike.
He had urged her to take the queen away:
"Unless you go, there will be punishment for me.
Stop your weeping and sadness.
When one has karma to suffer it's unfortunate,
but don't put the people in danger."

Hearing those words,
the queen, feeling all energy squeezed from her, gave a
    loud cry:
"Everything is so impermanent, I'll accept the trouble
and not cause others to suffer.

I thought I could delay.
But when I have no favor in the court,
I can only follow my turn of fate.
The maids must not have to suffer."

(sorrowful music)

So saying, she carried her little son.[71]
Her tears dropped like rain.
She cried loudly to the king:
"I who must suffer will leave.
Look at my face and remember it well,
for you will not see it again.
I'll not return, so do not wonder.
I shall no longer serve you.[72]
If there is anything I've done wrong
in the past, anything that displeased you,
I beg your pardon.
Let it not go on into another existence.[73]
I wish you long life,[74]
with no illness.
You don't look out of the golden curtains.
You're silent as though you don't care about me.
Because you are silent, they[75] can tell me it's time to go.
I'm sorry that you have cut me off from you so you no
    longer look upon my face."
Having spoken, Chanthewi paid respect and went away.
The maids of the right and the left followed her.
"Wait here, maids,

Since I have little left from good deeds, we cannot stay
    together.[76]
I used to let you do everything for me;
let us forgive, so nothing will add to our future mis-
    fortunes."
As she spoke she lifted her son.
Chantha nodded her head to her maid.
Crying, Chanthewi departed.
Chantha's maid led her away.

*(The maids ad-lib, accompanied by music indicating a person
of high status is leaving.)*

At once,
a soldier who was of the same heart as Chantha
received the queen,
and the maid went back to court.
The soldiers drank liquor,
no longer fearful and shy but haughty:
"We urge you to come and leave the court.
You've received orders. Why are you slow?
You'll make trouble for the soldiers too.
When you were queen, you never recognized us."
But another soldier, who was wiser, said,
"You need not speak like that."
They urged her to get into the boat.
Quickly they turned the prow away from the palace.
They went on for fifteen days with many troubles,
far away to find a place where there were no people.

(Fast music indicates people are hurrying away.)

When he had gone far with Chanthewi,
who looked so pitiful and was homeless,
the soldier who'd accepted the bribe
was at his wit's end, for many others were with him.
He wanted to kill Chanthewi but could not,
so he pretended, saying,
"Since she must surely die,
I'll try to strike with my sword."
His friends held him back:
"You can't do such a wrong; don't go beyond orders.
In respect to the queen's karma,
your great wrong will bring us trouble.
If you don't think of yourself and fear karma,
the turn of fate may easily cause you to suffer.
Whether she's bad or good, she was our mistress.
If we do wrong it'll not go well with us.
It's better for us to return home."
After speaking, the wise soldier said farewell to the queen.
Other soldiers who had pity and were kind
gave her rice and other things she'd need.
Then the boat moved out into the river.
Some looked at her, had pity, and felt sad.
The soldier who was evil
felt so thwarted that he didn't say farewell to his former
    queen.

(fast music, as between the last two verses)

Then
the queen, crying, found herself in a great forest.
As she came up from the river landing,
she knew not where to go.
Walking along, she carried her son:
"Look how I am suffering, my boy.
I have never walked in the forest before.
Because of my past bad deeds, my beloved has been born
    like this.
If you were a human being, you could be a friend.
I have a son, but it seems I have none at all.
I am following this path because evil Chantha
and the astrologer planned together.
And the maid joined in the plot.
She urged me to go far.
As for the soldier, he was going to kill me.
It is amazing that this could happen.
I think the Royal One whose room I shared still loves me.
Why do they not fear the king?
He was deceived by magic, I am sure."
Walking on, she cried.
The sounds of tigers, elephants, and deer
frightened her and shook her spirit.
Holding her child close, she cried and fled.
Chanthewi carried the shell as she went.

(music indicating a person of high status is going into the forest)

Walking along

in the hot sunlight,
she saw a forest cottage.
The queen joyously ran toward it.
She met two old people planting beans and sesame.
She sat down and greeted them with quick enthusiasm.
The two old people looked at each other.
Instantly, grandmother asked grandfather:
"Old man, is this good or bad? Are you honest with me?
I think I am not mistaken:
You had an appointment here with her. Speak!
Have you given your heart to this woman?
Look at her, her figure's like a bird-maiden's."[77]
Old grandmother threw her husband a fearsome glance[78]
    and her body trembled.
In his anger at the old woman, grandfather took a stick
    to strike her:
"What gave you such an idea?
She is the age of a granddaughter; don't go on so!
Lady, be not angry with my old woman, for she is out
    of her head.
Where do you come from?
Speak and make it clear to us."
The queen told her story from beginning to end.
The old people took her home.
Arranging the place for her quickly,
with pity and great kindness.

*(Music indicating movements of a person of high status accom-
panies ad-libbing by Queen Chanthewi and the old people.)*

Then
the lady, Chanthewi,
stayed five years with the old couple.
She was troubled more and more as time went by.
In the evening she pounded rice and carried water.
At dawn she went into the forest
to gather vegetables and kindling to light fires.
Some of these she sold to get the things she needed.
She took up her little son, a shell:
"I'm at the end of my strength, my beloved.
I've looked after you so that you could be a friend.
But you don't help your mother at all.[79]
You should be a person, dear son,
for you are already five or six years old. Aren't you, child?
At this age you should be happy and admired.
Child, you should lighten mother's burdens."
The lady could not sleep.
At dawn the sun rose and shone brightly.
She laid the child aside while she made preparations.
Dragging out a woven tray and putting it on the ground,
She put rice out to dry[80] and asked the old woman to look after it.
Taking up her carrying stick,[81] she went into the forest.
Going back and forth to gather vegetables and grasses as usual,
the beautiful lady searched for the things she needed.

(music for a person in the forest)

Now I'd like to tell
of a good spirit living in the trees.[82]
He pitied Chanthewi.
She was tired from all her hardships.
He knew the deity who had descended to be born as a
    human
was not like other people.
He had much merit
and would be great and renowned in the end.
If he fell in the water, he wouldn't be carried away by the
    current.
If he fell in the fire, he would not be burned.[83]
He would govern the kingdom and be famous,
known on earth, in heaven, and under the ground.[84]
He and the lady Rochana would be a happy couple.[85]
His mother would have happiness and well-being.
If the good spirit of the trees ignored all this, the mother's
    hardships would long continue.
He would have to make her son, who now hid himself,
    appear.
So the tree spirit miraculously made himself into a flock
    of wild chickens.
Quickly they began to eat the mother's rice.
Loudly they crowed, fought, and crowed again,
scratching and scattering the rice in the dirt.

(Music indicates an important magical transformation.)

Then

Prince Sang, still hidden, knew all.[86]
His mother had gone as usual to the forest.
In his heart, he had always thought:
"I want to go out and help Mother.
I have great pity for her.
Tired from physical hardships,
she comes back in the evening and cries.
Even though her small child is a shell,
she holds me and shows her affection for me.
Mother does more for me than anyone in the three
  worlds.
I would go out and show myself, but I'm afraid some-
  thing might happen.
The wild chickens have just come to eat the rice
of my mother and are making a loud noise.
They scratch and scatter it on the ground.
If Mother comes and sees it, she will cry."
Peering out through a little hole, he looked to right and
  left
to see if anyone was about, but he found no one.
Quickly, he got out of the shell.
He snatched a stick, ran after the chickens, and hit them.

(sound of small brass clappers)

He gathered together the rice spilled on the ground.
He turned, disappeared, moved a bit, and darted away.
If he should turn and see his mother,
he would flee back into the shell.

He boiled rice, fried fish, and waited for his mother.
He looked about and arranged everything.
He helped to chase away the wild chickens as the poor
    must do.
Absorbed in play, he was still watchful.

(ad-lib accompanied by small brass clappers)

Then
the mother felt in her heart
that she missed her little shell-child.
Walking a bit further, she soon came
to where she could gather kindling, vegetables, and
    roots;
everything there was to eat in the woods.
She carried her stick and baskets back,
quickly reaching the cottage.

(music for walking in the forest)

Then[87] she saw her beloved child.
"Whose child was ever like this one?"
He sat and played at the door of the cottage.
His face was like the beautiful moon floating in the sky.[88]
Prince Sang looked and saw his mother.
Startled, he ran back into the shell.
He was truly terrified.
Sadly, he waited to hear what his mother would say.
She laid aside her carrying stick and came closer.

Thinking it all very unusual, she looked around the room.
Hurriedly, she searched for the boy.
Not seeing him, she felt very strange:
"Perhaps the spirit of the house,[89] who is a troublesome
    friend,
came to play and tease me.
That is why he has disappeared."
Thoughts circled in the mind of the lady.
Cooked rice and fish . . . everything was put in order.
She thought it very strange.
She looked at the rice first,
then asked the old man and woman.
She did not eat the rice and fish.
The queen thought and thought again:
"I will wait and see to know for sure."
She held the shell, not thinking she had seen her son.
She thought and looked around, and lovingly lifted the
    shell high.
Tears came from her eyes.
At dawn when the sun was up,
she pretended to look for her baskets and carrying stick.
Going down from the cottage, she looked around.
Walking softly, she picked up a stick not far from the
    house.
In a hidden place she watched for a long time.
The woman was patient and silent.

Then
the prince looked out of his shell,

He did not see his mother,
hidden behind a wall, and thought there was no one
about.
It was quiet; no one spoke.
Stealthily, he came out and walked away.
He sat outside the cottage feeling very comfortable.
Picking up pebbles and sand, he played, forgetting him-
self.
His mother, hidden, saw it all:
"Oh, oh, my dear son!
Hidden, you stayed in the shell.
Beloved of your mother, marvelous person."
She walked into the hut, picked up a stick,
and broke the shell into pieces as small as powder.
Prince Sang was alarmed as though he'd been held up to
a fire.[90]
He wanted to flee into the shell but was thwarted.

(fast sound of brass clappers)

Embracing the feet of his mother,
he bowed his head and cried.
"Mother broke the shell in little pieces,"
he cried on and on sadly:
"It is as though my mother had killed me.
She doesn't love me even a little.
Mother broke the shell and she has broken my life.
She will not have long to love me."

Listening to her child
the mother felt more and more desolate.
She kissed and stroked his eyes and head:
"Shall we not stay together, beloved? Why do you speak
    so?
The end of misfortune and the consequences of bad
    deeds has come.[91]
Son, do not say anything to frighten your mother.
I have met misfortune and hardships,
because that shell was evil.
It covered my dear son,
making it possible for the astrologer to speak against me,
and your father to be deceived by an evil woman.
Without delay, we shall go back to court.
After so many troubles, we see each other's faces, mother
    and child.
Don't cry and be bound up in your thoughts of the
    shell,
nor love it so much, for it was not permanent.
Such a shell is so common and plentiful."
Saying enough for the moment, she called the old man
    and woman,
and told them the whole story
from the beginning to the end.
Both wondered, not believing the lady.

Then
the old man and woman began to marvel.

Together they went into the cottage with the lady
and saw the figure of the prince.
They were startled, as though their bodies were frozen:
"The beloved's face is so very beautiful.
He is our merit.[92]
Since our birth, we have heard of no one like this.
This is the first time we have met or seen such a one,
    truly.
Is it your child, lady? Really?
What great merit and honor!
Oh, how was such a figure made?[93]
For generations
no one has seen such a one."
The old man and woman kissed and stroked the boy.
The two were very happy.

1. *The people cried out that he must have a son.*

2. *Bowing respectfully, they prayed together.*

3. *The deity was startled. . . . He knew in his heart he would die.*

4. *"Look into my dream."*

5. *"Your daughter will not betray you."*

6. "If I don't reverse my prophecy, [the] . . . gold must be returned."

7. *"But I ask the favor of delay to lie by the fire just for seven days."*

8. *They went . . . far away to find a place where there were no people.*

9. *Chanthewi carried the shell as she went.*

10. *"Have you given your heart to this woman?"*

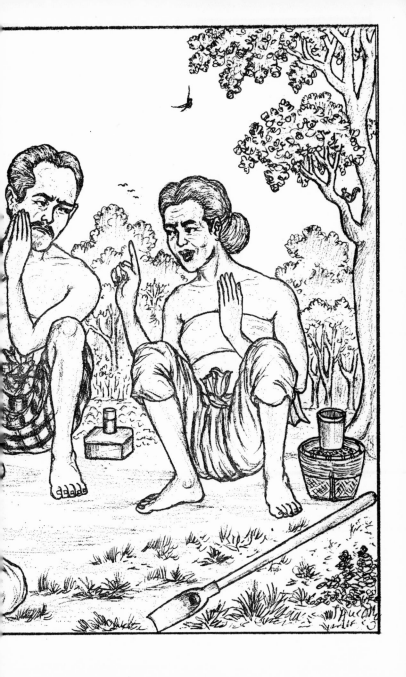

11. *In the evening she pounded rice and carried water.*

12. *Taking up her carrying stick, she went into the forest.*

13. *Picking up pebbles and sand, he played, forgetting himself.*

List of Characters
(in order of appearance)

ACTS TWO TO NINE

(in addition to King Yosawimon, Queen Chanthewi, Queen Chantha, the old man and woman, and Prince Sang)

PRINCESS CHANTHI, daughter of Queen Chantha
OLD WOMAN OF SUMETHA, brewer of love-potions
SERPENT-KING, ruler of an underwater kingdom
QUEEN PHANTHURAT, ruler of the ogres
KING SAMON, ruler of the kingdom of Samon
QUEEN MONTHA, wife of King Samon
PRINCESS ROCHANA, maiden destined from a former existence to be the wife of Prince Sang; daughter of King Samon
A NEGRITO, Prince Sang in disguise
INDRA, high deity moved by the sufferings of Rochana and Chanthewi
WISANUKAM, messenger of Indra

The Drowning of Prince Sang

Though years passed, Yosawimon thought only of his beloved Chanthewi, asking, "Oh, in what past life were the evil deeds done that made me lose both wife and child?"

Chantha, vexed that the king did not love her and cause her to rise like a cloud above all others in the court, schemed again with her maid. Together they instructed Chantha's little daughter to go to the king and plead that he once promised that a child born to any of his wives would inherit the kingdom. When little Chanthi suggested to King Yosawimon that the promise might be fulfilled if her mother were raised to the position of first queen, the king felt pained as though pierced by a spear. Sensing that Chantha had taught the little girl the words she spoke, he lashed out at the woman, saying, "With great ambition you tried to take the sun." Chantha responded cleverly by sharing the king's anger at her daughter:

"Who taught you to speak like this? No matter how much I pinch and slap you, you don't remember, but pick up what they say everywhere."

Then, to the king, she affirmed:

"If you think I wished to destroy Chanthewi, I ask

111

to be beaten to find out the truth, and my flesh rubbed with salt for the crows to eat. I would be the enemy of the kingdom."

Though the king, absorbed in anger and worry, ordered Chantha to go, she pressed on, saying, "You chase me away as though I were a marble stuck in your throat, because you still think of Chanthewi."

The king, struck by Chantha's haughtiness, berated her:

"You speak beyond your station, not even fearing death. As though you were the lizard who received gold, you lift your head with such dignity."[1] Filled with wrath, he struck at her with his sword.

Miserable with the failure of her first scheme, Chantha returned to her room and sent her maid to the old woman Sumetha, who was skilled in making love-potions.

When the maid went up on the old woman's porch she spoke sweetly, saying, "The trip to you was slow and long, but my merit helped me to find you."

The old woman, gleaning from the maid's story that she would be highly rewarded, picked up her sack of medicines with her scarf, and went to the door to see if the wind was right for good results. Satisfied, she accompanied the maid to the inner court of the palace where Chantha alone awaited her in the dark of the night.

Assuring Chantha that magic could make the king love her beyond all reason, the old woman took from her medicine sack two skulls with ghostly power.[2] Placing them on an offering tray, she lit candles and performed a ceremony which caused both skulls to rise. She held a candle under the chin of one and collected in a cosmetic jar the oil that dripped from it. With the beeswax which closed the mouth of one skull, she molded a figure of Chantha and the king embracing each other. These figures she tied with a cord used for binding a corpse, and put them under Chantha's mattress. She lit a candlewick after putting the king's name on it, saying: "At midnight let his passion bring him here." She instructed Chantha to give the king charmed betel[3] to chew. After teaching her magic words to breathe on the king, the old woman left Chantha to bathe and rub her body with powder made from the oil collected in the cosmetic jar.

The old woman's potion made the king's heart burn like a fire. Reposing in a chair was like lying on strips of flattened bamboo with thorns. When a breeze blew through the window, the odor of Chantha's oil-powder was more fragrant than flowers from heaven.

He went to Chantha, who feigned sleep as she lay beside her daughter. Gently he told her he had wronged her and tried to elicit a response of love from her. Chantha could pretend no longer when her daughter awoke and found her father when she sought comfort from her mother's breast. Urging the little girl to go back to sleep, Chantha said:

"Large cats walk on the railing: there are a thousand. Go to sleep, or they will eat your liver!"[4] She called her trusted maid to take away the child and swing her to sleep in her cradle.

Mingling anger and sweetness, Chantha still held the king at bay. Mad with passion and remorse for the wrong he had done her, he swore, "I will lie down and let you slice my flesh."

Then Chantha gave in and they were as intimate as they wished with each other. All sense of displeasure and danger left them.

The next morning Chantha convinced the king that the evil shell had become a person who would later become a rebel against the kingdom. His face still darkened by the love-potion that made him believe all that Chantha said was true, the king ordered soldiers to go into the forest and kill the boy, whom he now believed to be another man's son.

Coming to the forest house of Chanthewi, a soldier recognized her, though she was thin, with her clothing patched everywhere. Her body, showing through torn places, gave an appearance of desolation. On seeing the boy, a soldier observed from his hiding place:

"He is the king's son, surely there is no question. What can we say? It is most disturbing. He is so handsome, close to his mother, asking for things so sweetly and chatting." Waiting until the queen had gone into the forest to hunt for herbs and firewood, the soldier approached the boy and tried to lure him closer with promises of a toy.

The little boy responded:

"Is it really pretty? I'd like to see it. If you're going to give it to me, put it in my hand."

The soldier grabbed the outstretched hand. He tried in many ways to kill the boy, whose merit continued to protect him. Finally the soldier took him back to the palace, where he was put into chains and imprisoned.

Upon her return from the forest, Chanthewi heard from the old man and woman that, while they were fearfully hiding, a soldier had taken her son away. Distraught, she started the long journey on foot back to the court, arriving just as Chantha had convinced the king that the boy should be drowned. Upon seeing Chanthewi, the king changed his mind and told a guard to bring the boy to him. The quick Chantha, however, had already given the order to another soldier to take the boy away and throw him into the water with a heavy stone tied to his body. Discovering too late that the deed had been done, Chanthewi and the king both fainted.

Chantha brought Yosawimon to consciousness, breathing love-magic on him as she said, "If Prince Sang had merit he could not die, but since he has sunk, there is no reason to be sad." The king was again under the spell of Chantha's love-magic.

Country folk revived Chanthewi, trying to comfort her, saying, "He is dead; there is nothing to do."

Chanthewi returned to the old man and woman.

As he was sinking, Prince Sang cried for his mother and pitied her, "She needs someone to help look after the cottage," he thought. Although he fainted in the water, he did not die; slowly he sank to the world of the serpents.[5]

The Boyhood of Prince Sang

The king of the serpents felt uncomfortably warm. Though he was afraid of the *garuda* bird,[6] he emerged from his palace. Seeing Prince Sang at the bottom of the sea with a stone attached to his body, he felt sure the child was dead. "Why did anyone kill a little one like this?" he asked.

Pitying the boy, he picked him up and saw a sign on the palm of his hand which led him to believe this child was a being of great merit. The serpent-king took Prince Sang back to his palace and prayed: "If, from a past life, this child and I have merit which can help each other, then let him not die."

As the serpent-king gently rubbed magic water on the boy's body, Prince Sang regained consciousness. Thinking the serpent a person, Prince Sang greeted him respectfully and explained all that had happened, asking him to help find his [Prince Sang's] mother. For a time Prince Sang stayed with the serpent-king and queen. Knowing that the boy could not stay forever under water, the serpent-king planned to send him to the kingdom of the ogres,[7] where Phanthurat, a childless widow, was queen. The serpent-king explained that he was not human, but would always help if the boy needed him.

He dressed the child beautifully and took him to the surface of the water. In a golden boat given by the serpent-king, Sang Thong set out to look for Phanthurat's kingdom. The serpent-king prayed that no ogre would eat Prince Sang before he reached Phanthurat and that the boat would drift only to her kingdom.

On the way Prince Sang saw man-eating fishes and, frightened, thought of his mother. Since he could not find her, it was as though they were separated by death: "But when I am old enough," he thought, "I shall look everywhere, until I find her."

The deities helped him to get to the kingdom of the ogres. Soldiers, guarding the shores, wanted to kill and eat him, but they could not touch the boat because of the serpent-king's prayers. When he came close, Prince Sang prayed and gave them a note from the serpent-king, which they took to Phanthurat.

Overjoyed that she had not been forgotten by the serpent-king and had been sent a son, Phanthurat asked many of the ogres if it would be good for her to raise the boy as her son. None found any objection except a fortune-teller, who warned:

"Do not do it. He is no child of the serpent-king. He is a human. For ogres and men to love each other is very difficult. It is the same as a bird that leaves eggs in another bird's nest. The small birds, after being hatched in the second nest, will return to the first. Or it will befall as between Phra Rot and Nang Meri."[8]

Angry with the fortune-teller, Phanthurat felt he was

not telling the truth, but spoke as he did because he was afraid that the boy, as her son, might become more powerful than he in later years. Besides, she reasoned, it would be a different kind of love between her and the boy. Why say it would be like the love between Phra Rot and Nang Meri?

None of the other ogres objected, and Phanthurat commanded them to assume the bodies of humans. Going to the sea to find the boat, she prayed that if Prince Sang had merit, his boat would float to her. She paid respect three times as she prayed. The boat floated in to shore and Phanthurat lifted the little boy out happily. The boat disappeared as it went out to sea again. Taking him back to the court, Phanthurat asked the boy his name and birthplace. Crying, he explained all to her. She pitied him and comforted him, saying, "Don't be sad. I will raise you as my own son."

Phanthurat ordered her attendants to make the palace beautiful to celebrate Prince Sang's arrival. She told them to dress him and make preparations for a welcoming ceremony.[9] She fanned smoke from a candle toward him to bring back his sense of well-being and put magic dots on his forehead to protect him from sickness and pain.

The festivities, including wrestling, *lakhon* [dance-drama], *khon* [masked play], walking on tightropes, firecrackers, Mon dancing, and Chinese drama, lasted seven days and seven nights.[10]

Phanthurat arranged for maids to look after the boy

and to play lullabies for him on stringed instruments. She gave him the right to beat or kill anyone who would not obey him.

Sang Thong stayed with Phanthurat for fifteen years. As she watched him grow up, she was very happy. However, she had to go into the forest for fresh meat—elephant, tiger, and deer, which she killed, washed, and ate. Always she feared that when she left the palace, he might flee. For this reason she never told him exactly how long she would be gone. If she said "seven days," she would come back at nightfall; but, if she said "a day," she would stay for several.

She forbade Prince Sang to go to the wells on the right and left sides of the palace; nor was he allowed to go into a room next to the sleeping room.

One day, while waiting for Phanthurat to return, Prince Sang decided to enter these forbidden places. In the room, he found bones of tigers, lions, and humans. Terribly frightened, he looked for the wells. When he opened the left well and put in his finger, silver stuck to it. When he opened the well to the right, it shone beautifully. Gold stuck to his finger. He tried to wipe it off so that Phanthurat would not see it, but he could not. He put a cloth around the finger so Phanthurat would think he had hurt it. Seeking a place to hide in another part of the palace, he found the disguise of a Negrito,[11] crystal shoes, and a stick. When he put them on, he found he could fly, even out the window. Afraid his mother would come back, he put them away.

Realizing that Phanthurat was an ogress, Prince Sang planned that he would flee to find his own mother. He felt that he could not trust the ogress and might die without finding his original mother. On the other hand, he had never repaid the kindness of his ogress mother. Such thoughts brought tears to his eyes, but he wiped them away so the maids would not see.

Phanthurat stayed in the forest for seven days. Missing her son, she hurried back. Holding and stroking him, she noticed the white cloth tied on his finger. When she questioned him, he replied that he had cut his hand with a knife and it had needed a bandage to stop the bleeding. Angry with the maids for allowing her son to hurt himself, Phanthurat ordered that they be flailed. Prince Sang urged restraint, saying they had forbidden him the knife, but he had used it anyway.

The Flight of Prince Sang

Since Phanthurat's merit was at an end, the time had come for her to die.

After telling Prince Sang that she would go into the forest for the day, she told the maids to look after him well and not make him angry. While the maids were asleep, the boy fled and immersed himself in the well of gold. From the palace he took the Negrito disguise, crystal shoes, and stick. Sadly he thought of Phanthurat, who had done him much good which he had not returned. If he did not die, he thought, he would some day return to her. Crying with pity for the woman who had loved him, he put on the disguise and shoes, took the stick, and flew away.

When he had flown for seven nights, he came to a large mountain. Tired, he rested under a tall tree.

When the maids awoke and did not find Prince Sang, they cried fearfully, for they felt that guarding the boy was as fearsome a duty as guarding a king's treasure.

Upon her return Phanthurat called for Prince Sang, but there was no answer. She was overcome by a feeling of fear and strangeness. The well of gold, she found, was shallower. Discovering that the Negrito disguise and the crystal shoes were missing, she knew that Prince

Sang had gone. She hurried to sound the alarm gong, which brought all the ogres to her. Asked to help their queen find Prince Sang, they flew off in such numbers that they darkened the sun.

From the top of the mountain, Prince Sang saw the darkness, heard the sound, and knew that the ogres were following him. Taking off the disguise and shoes, he climbed the tree, hoping his golden skin would make the ogres think him the spirit of the tree. As they rushed by, they asked, "Spirit, have you seen a being disguised as a Negrito?" Prince Sang pointed in another direction and all the ogres went that way. Prince Sang prayed: "By my mother's merit, do not let the ogress-queen climb the mountain."

Coming quickly with her servants, Phanthurat saw Prince Sang in the tree. Laughing and crying at the same time, she clapped her hands.

"Why are you there? Come down. I won't beat you," she called. But Prince Sang would not climb down. Because Prince Sang had prayed, Phanthurat fell whenever she tried to climb.

"I have looked after you and you do not remember it. My heart will break," cried the ogress-queen.

"You have done me good as has no one else in the world," answered Prince Sang. "I leave not because I'm angry but because I must find my mother who has no place to go. I don't know whether she is dead or alive, but I shall seek her everywhere. Don't be angry with me, for soon I'll return."

"You're not likely to come back," Phanthurat cried. "It is not because you want to follow your mother, but because you don't want to stay with me. If you want to go and it will make you happy, I'll not forbid it, but come down for just a little while so I can admire you. Don't be afraid, though I am an ogress. You may stay or go with my blessing. I give you the disguise, shoes, and stick, which have magic power. I will give you another bit of magic—a chant to call animals, and fish, even the powerful *garuda* bird. Everything you need will come at your will. If you go, I cannot live. Come down quickly to get the words before I die."

Prince Sang was very sad, but afraid that if he went down Phanthurat might catch him.

"Don't be unhappy," he said. "I'm very tired and can't go down. Let me stay up here in comfort for a while. The sun is getting hot at noonday. When it sets, I'll go down. I would like to have your magic. If you want to give it to me, write it on the ground where you stand and I'll go down to learn it."

Phanthurat did not know what to do. Looking up at Prince Sang, she cried:

"What karma do I have to make you do this? I tried to look after you, but now you won't come to me. I must be at the end of my merit and I must die. When I am dead, will you burn my lifeless body? Come down, learn by yourself the magic I have written."

She cried until, brokenhearted, she died.

When her attendants saw Phanthurat die, they too cried.

Prince Sang hurried down, thinking of all she had done for him. Not to have repaid this kindness and to have caused her death were great wrongs. He ordered the attendants to take her body back to the city and make proper preparations for the cremation to be held when he returned.

Prince Sang learned the magic, put on the disguise and shoes, and flew away. When he reached Samon,[12] he did not know whose kingdom it might be. Children who had eaten their breakfast and were chasing the cattle out to pasture found him sitting on the edge of a paddy field.[13] Was he mad? Everything about him seemed very strange to them. Was he an Indian sailor?

"Don't trust him, he may eat our insides," said one.

"He is a very big monkey," said another.

"If he's a monkey, why has he no tail?" a third asked. "His face is very funny."

"Maybe he's a ghost of the fields," suggested another.

One boy was not afraid. Laughing, he said, "He is a Negrito who won't harm us. . . . Come, play with us."

When lunchtime came, they took out their rice and shared it with the Negrito. At dusk the children invited him home, but he refused, so they suggested that he stay in the fields and play with them later.

The Choice of Husbands

The king of Samon, feeling he would become "hurt, aching, feverish, and old, with lessening strength each year,"[14] wanted to find husbands for his seven daughters. "If I can find a son-in-law with merit," he said to his wife, "I shall give the kingdom to him."

He sent messengers to all the lands paying tribute to him, telling them to send their princes to vie for the hands of his daughters, who would choose their favorites. Feelings were high in the kingdom. Kings who had no sons sent their nephews. If their sons were married, the fathers urged them to put aside their wives and seek a powerful king's daughter. Some of the men dressed in gold and thought no one could beat them. Some thought of love-magic to charm a king's daughter; some went to astrologers to find the auspicious time according to the stars. Others thought it depended on their merit, so why worry?

In the morning they appeared in the courtyard of the palace. The king urged his queen to look out the window and see them. Some were handsome; some were not.

The queen bathed her daughters, rubbing turmeric on the girls' skins to make them beautiful. They went to the king, who urged them to choose their husbands, throwing garlands to those they chose. The girls were shy, not wanting to go out. They lowered their heads and picked at the woven mat on which they sat.

"Today is a great day. Go," urged both the king and queen.

The girls went out with their nurses, afraid to go on, yet afraid to go back. When they reached the place where the young men stood, they hid behind the curtain.

All the princes were eager to see the princesses. They complained to each other about the long wait, yet all sat smiling. They stretched to see if the girls were coming, and courtiers jested that they were like people who had never seen court women.

The girls came out with their nurses, peering out from behind them. When the princes saw how shy the girls were, some raised their eyebrows; others coughed with embarrassment. Some tried to keep others from seeing the girls.

Though all the older sisters threw their garlands, Rochana,[15] the youngest, chose no one. Returning to her father, she told him that she did not want to marry but chose to stay with her parents until she died. When the king saw that his daughter liked none of the princes, he lost strength. Trying to persuade her that she must choose a husband before he became feeble, he argued that all the princes had status and were handsome. Suggesting the proper relationship of a daughter to a father, he asserted that she had not yet pleased him and put an end to his worries.

The king suggested to his wife that he choose for Rochana so that she could be married with her sisters. The queen was not pleased with this solution, for she feared that Rochana would be unhappy, do something wrong, and bring dishonor to her parents. She suggested that the king invite all the men of the kingdom, young and old, for Rochana's choice. Pleased with her suggestion, the king gave orders for everyone, though he be poor, or lacking arms and legs, to come to the palace.

The chosen princes were very happy, laughing and teasing those who, overlooked, sat dejectedly. The chosen suggested to the others that they had no merit.

In the countryside, men who had gambled away their money borrowed clothes from friends to go to court. Some cut their hair very short; others put oil on theirs to make it stand straight up. Many did not sleep all night, trying to dress themselves. When their wives would not help them, they swore at them. Some were so old they walked with a stick, yet all went to court.

When the men of the kingdom were all assembled, the king called Rochana out. Though she looked at them all—young and old, rich and poor—she liked none. Again she told the king that she would rather stay with him than marry: "In the future, if I do anything wrong, you can kill me."

ACT SIX

The Winning of Rochana

Feeling at his wits' end, King Samon sat holding both knees.[16] When he asked the soldiers if all the men had come from town and country, they told him there was no one left but a Negrito who seemed to know nothing. With great anger in his heart, the king suggested to his wife that Rochana might love the Negrito.

Ordered by the king, soldiers went to the fields to find the Negrito. When he showed no interest in going to the palace, the soldiers tried to drag him back but were not strong enough. One tried to make him laugh; all were afraid of him.

The children who looked after the buffaloes were angry when the soldiers touched the Negrito, and asked where they were taking him. Explaining that they followed the king's orders, the soldiers warned them they would suffer if they made the task difficult. "If you help we'll give you cakes, delicious cakes from the court," they urged.

The children all spoke at once to get the cakes, saying, "It'll do no good to try to take him like that . . . but if you pick some red flowers, he'll follow."

The soldiers happily gathered the flowers, stringing them on a long stick. The Negrito followed.

128

At court everyone laughed at him. The king said to Rochana, "Perhaps you'll choose the Negrito, since others aren't good enough for you."

As though there were a divine being in her heart, Rochana wanted to go out and see the Negrito. She felt no shyness.

Appearing disinterested when he saw Rochana, the Negrito prayed that if in a past life he and Rochana had made merit together, she would see his golden body inside the Negrito disguise. As he prayed, Rochana saw the golden body and thought it was her merit that made her see. She prayed that if from a past existence they were a couple meant to be together, the garland that she threw carelessly would be caught on his arm. When she tossed it, the garland fell as she prayed. The nurses, on the other hand, felt misdeeds from her past life made her throw the garland.

When the king found that Rochana had thrown her garland to the Negrito, he fainted. Queen Montha supported him and brought him back to consciousness. Stamping his foot, he damned his daughter, threatening to beat her, but Montha forbade it. To her daughter, Montha said:

"You have no love of your status. Everyone will gossip about you until you die. You have made me so ashamed."

Rochana was afraid to say what she had seen, and only replied, "It was my karma that made me choose."

She was hardly able to speak, feeling that water was flooding her mouth. Yet she begged pardon of her father and mother. She told her mother she must stay with the Negrito until the results of her karma were over, though she hoped her mother would not be unhappy.

In his heart, the king loved and hated his daughter. He tried to control his anger, thinking perhaps he could trick the Negrito. He ordered the soldiers to build a field hut for Rochana and the Negrito to live in:

"At first I wanted all my daughters to marry at once, but Rochana preferred not to marry. So she and the Negrito need not marry but can simply live in the hut. Let them stay together during these nights of the fourth month of the year of the tiger."[17]

The soldiers went out to cut bamboo for the hut. For furnishings they took a mat, a mosquito net, a mattress, a rice pot, and a large clay jar for water.

When the six other daughters learned that Rochana had chosen the Negrito, they were angry at her for making them ashamed.

"In this life you have done just right, nothing wrong," they said sarcastically. "You have chosen a husband who is handsome. His body is like a dead tree! His stomach is big and his back is long. He is quite suitable for Rochana. His eyes and ears are like a big cat's."

Though they talked on, Rochana was not ashamed.

"Can you make a potion to get the Negrito's love?" one asked.

They all said they would like to beat her:

"We never want to see you again.[18] You will have no sisters," they told her.

"Everyone will think your husbands are very good. They have much merit. Their bodies will be delectable," answered Rochana sarcastically. "In the future you'll all have much, but I'll not ask your help. Father gave us each a choice, but when I made mine, you came to criticize me. We're all of the same mother, but you don't speak suitably to me."

At last the six sisters felt they could not match Rochana's words. In fact, they said, their jaws were weary.

The soldiers who had built the hut told Rochana that all was ready. When her father ordered her to go, she was very sad. She went to her mother and said:

"You've done so much for me.[19] You've looked after me since I was little. I've always been happy with you. I want to make you happy, but I've done wrong and made you ashamed. Karma forces me to go. I'll return and pay back what you've done for me."

Rochana cried on and on. Listening to her, Montha pitied her child. She felt both love and anger. There were tears in her eyes.

The Negrito motioned to Rochana to come away. She paid respect to her mother, saying again that karma made her leave. Turning back and looking at the palace, she thought how happy she had always been there. When the Negrito looked at her, he saw she was crying, but she turned her face so he wouldn't see. She wiped away her tears, trying to love the Negrito and forget her hardships.

When they reached the hut, Rochana found it very

unpleasant and sat outside crying. But the Negrito picked up a utensil and tossed it as in a game the young play at the Songkran festival. He put water through a strainer and wet Rochana's hair.[20]

"I'm bored to death because you can't speak and don't know anything," complained Rochana.

Pretending he did not hear, the Negrito sat fanning himself. He took a pot which was not made for boiling rice, lit the fire, and put the rice into it. He put up the mosquito net, although it was still day. Sitting against a pillow and smiling broadly, he played with his feet.

When it was dark, he spoke as a lover to Rochana:

"Oh younger one, my love, beautiful as the moon. When your face is so sad, I don't like it. We were meant to be a happy couple. I used to live in a kingdom beyond the sky, far away in the Himalayas,[21] but a divinity brought me to you because we were destined from a past life to be together this time. Though I'm not as beautiful as you, a king's daughter, I must have merit to get such a beautiful wife." Then, with sarcasm, he continued, "Your father must have liked me very much to give me all these things. We're rich. Don't be unhappy. I'll try to keep you from feeling ashamed in front of your sisters and their husbands."

He urged her to come and sit in the hut with him. Thinking it all very funny, Rochana laughed with embarrassment. She tried to find work to keep herself from feeling uncomfortable. She chose a knife to prepare betel. When the Negrito called again, she turned slightly but sat quietly. Though she thought of the golden body she had seen when she threw the garland, she did not want to speak of it.

"You say we have great treasure," she said, "but we have nothing. Our home is like the nest of a crow or a wild chicken. This morning you couldn't speak, but now you talk very wisely. You speak sweetly and well. Your body is beautiful. Your eyes are as big as goose eggs, and your body's really like an ogre's. Father loves you very much to allow you to stay in this field hut. The garden tools he has given you are just right for you."

"Why do you speak to me like this?" asked the Negrito. "I'll not argue with you for it's true as you say. I'm not handsome, but . . . " he laughed, "women must love me, since you threw me your garland. I hope in the future you will find me handsome."

He invited her to go into the net, saying there were many mosquitoes about. Rochana replied that he made her laugh, for he spoke so smartly.

"I threw you the garland," she said, "not because I love you but because you like red flowers. Your body isn't handsome. I know you aren't a Negrito. Why do you appear like one? Why do you cover your beautiful body? You don't have to tease me. Because of your disguise my father chased us away. My unhappiness is as great as a mountain. I am ashamed before everyone. I don't want to sleep with the Negrito body. I'm afraid."

"Rochana, you are very wise," replied the Negrito. "True, the Negrito is not my true body. Never mind my beard; I can shave it off. I can comb my hair. Never mind my black body; I can bathe and shine it with tamarind fruit. I can rub it with white powder. As for my stomach, never mind. It's just that I eat much. I will dress as Rochana wishes."

He removed his Negrito disguise and put it in the closet. Then he came and sat beside Rochana, touching her where her breast cloth had fallen from her shoulder, so she would look at his body. Unaware that he had taken off the Negrito disguise, Rochana was about to slap away his hand. When she saw his beautiful body, she was startled. He was as handsome as a deity. She could not speak. "Why don't you go on criticizing me?" he asked, laughing. He led her into the room.

"If you pull my arm, it will part from my shoulder. You are as beautiful as a god," Rochana said. "Why did you dress as a Negrito?" Though he wished she would not go on, she continued, feeling both love and annoyance for him as she pouted: "If you had not worn the Negrito disguise, Father wouldn't have sent us from the city. It was the reason for my shame."

"Why are you still angry at the Negrito?" he asked. "I wore the disguise to find the woman who was truly meant to be with me through this life. Anyone who was not, would laugh at me. You were right in seeing that inside was the golden body."

He sat very close to her. She resisted him, saying, "I have less than I deserve, because you show me love without telling me whose son you are."

Then he explained that he was a prince named Sang Thong, and told her his story. That night they became husband and wife.

In the morning he again put on the Negrito disguise, saying to Rochana, "We are husband and wife, poor together. Let's help each other prepare our rice."

"I've never in my life prepared food," replied Rochana sadly. "I'm sorry but I can't do it. When I was in the court, it was always brought when I was hungry. I've never done anything. But if I must, I will."

They helped each other.

At night Prince Sang took off the Negrito disguise and hid it. She pleaded with him not to put it on again, but he only laughed at her.

Rochana planned that when he slept she would steal the disguise. She pushed back the sheet, invited him to lie down, and massaged him to sleep. As he slept he held her close; but stealthily she took his arms from around her and put a pillow in her place. She took the disguise to the kitchen and made a fire. Although she slashed it with a knife, it was the same as before. When she had hit it until she was tired, she became angry. She put the disguise into the fire, but it did not burn. In many ways she tried to destroy it, but without result.

Prince Sang dreamed of his wife as he hugged the pillow. Groping for her, he found he held only a pillow and was startled. After looking for Rochana, he looked for the Negrito disguise, but found nothing. When he saw the kitchen fire, he brought water to put it out.

"The Negrito disguise is mine, not yours," he said to Rochana. "Why do you burn it? Don't you respect me? Or if you want to play with it, put it on. You can be a lady Negrito. I'd like to beat you."

"If you kill me," Rochana replied, "I'll gladly die. When you put on the disguise, you shame me. That's why I tried to burn it."

They quarreled on as Prince Sang put on the disguise. He teased her by clapping his hands as he went into the sleeping room. Then he pretended, while still angry, to go to sleep.

Rochana followed him.

"I have done wrong, but must you go on being angry?" she asked. "We are husband and wife."

She stroked his body and his beard, and gave him betel to eat. Smiling, he said he was no longer angry. If, however, she tried to destroy his disguise again, he warned, he would remain angry. Yet he did not trust her and wore the Negrito disguise always.

As the days passed, she wove cloth while he sang to her of their love.[22]

❦ ACT SEVEN

Hunting and Fishing

King Samon looked for a way to kill the Negrito.

"I plan to give gifts to the divinities," he announced. "Tomorrow each son-in-law, including the Negrito, must bring back a hundred fish. I shall kill anyone who is late, or brings less than a hundred."

The soldiers hurried to the homes of the king's six daughters and their husbands, telling them to bring fish according to the royal order.

The men were happy, saying:

"There are many fish. Don't ask for only a hundred. If he wants a boatload, we can bring them. We pity only the Negrito. He'll take his wife to help him with a trap and net scoop until they are both weak and hungry. They'll have only tiny fish, so the king will be angry and kill him."

They called to their servants:

"Tomorrow we'll go before cockcrow. Prepare a boat with large and small nets."

The soldiers hurried away to the house of the Negrito. Staying outside the fence, for they feared the dog, they called. "Where is Rochana?"

Rochana was making torches so she could make blackened oil to smooth her face. Although poor and burdened with hardships, she tried to stay beautiful, powdering and dressing herself. She arranged her skirt neatly in folds[23] and gave food to her husband. Preparing betel, she cut such a hard piece that the knife broke. The Negrito rested, chanting verses with long, drawn-out sounds as he pulled hairs from his chin.[24]

When the soldier who had called to Rochana saw her, he cried with pity. After hearing the king's order, Rochana went into the hut and embraced the feet of her husband as she cried:

"You must surely die. If you do, I shall follow you. I'll never want a second husband."

Listening to her say this, he loved her even more and tried to comfort her:

"My beloved, don't be sad or you'll not be beautiful. Thank you for loving me. I could never find another woman like Rochana. Don't worry, I can find more fish than the king asks. Now go to sleep. Although I go alone, I can catch them and am not afraid of the others."

In the morning Prince Sang took leave of Rochana. Taking his magic stick and shoes, he flew to the side of a stream. He stopped in a banyan tree and took off the Negrito disguise. He prayed that through the power of his ogress mother all the fish in the surrounding waters would come together.

Meanwhile the other sons-in-law called their many servants to go fishing. The royal daughters prepared food. The men and servants prepared nets, hook and lines, basket traps; but they caught only a crocodile.

Catching nothing, they were astonished. Their boat floated to where Prince Sang sat surrounded by fish. Thinking he was a deity, they paid homage. Prince Sang smiled inwardly, pretending not to know them:

"Who are you and where are you going? You have good faces, but have you come to steal my fish? You don't know who I am. I am a deity who has killed many people. Speak. Why have you come?"

The six were terrified, for they thought he was Lord of the Forest. They paid respect, raising their hands very high in fear of his power:

"The king makes us compete with the Negrito at fishing. We've thrown our nets from early in the morning; yet we have no fish, probably because of bad luck. Now we're discouraged, hungry, and tired. If we lose to the Negrito we'll be shamed. The king will kill us: we are only sad that our wives will be widows. As a divinity, you look after many fish. Please give us fish to save us."

Prince Sang laughed when he heard them, saying they were out of their minds:

"You don't fear karma when you go fishing? But since you ask I'll give some of them to you. However, I'm going to ask for something. You can give or not. Discuss it among yourselves."

Enthusiastically they accepted his words:

"What do you ask? Everything we have that you want, we will give—ducks, chickens, liquor, rice, bananas, sugar cane, cakes."

Then Prince Sang said:

"I am a powerful deity. I don't need food to eat. I ask for the ends of your noses. As usual, I ask only a little of each. If you give them, I will give the fish."

When the men heard this they sat and discussed it:

"Eh, the deity is full of cunning to exchange fish for the ends of people's noses."

"Our wives will see our short noses and be angry, turning their backs on us."

"Don't think about it," said one. "Stand the pain; don't complain. We've hunted for fish everywhere and there are none. If the Negrito finds them, we'll be embarrassed."

Hesitating, they lowered their heads and glanced at each other. All agreed not to be afraid of the pain. One snatched the knife of a servant, and handed it to the divinity.

Prince Sang smiled, asking, "Why are you cowards, like little fishes?"

He sharpened the knife on a stone, while all waited fearfully. Holding each nose-tip between his two fingers, he asked, "Shall I take it?" and then cut.

The six men looked at each other's wounds. The husband of the eldest sister pretended it was all funny but whispered to the others, "Ask for the fish!"

Prince Sang prayed: "Let all the fish who are about to die come up on the bank to be divided among the brothers-in-law."[25]

Many fish came up and died. Prince Sang gave each

man two and told them to go. Paying respect to the deity, they strung the fish together and rowed their boat away.

When they had gone, Prince Sang put on the Negrito disguise. He put the remaining fish on a string over a carrying stick before he flew home.

When he was near the fields and his hut, he flew earthward. He climbed the ladder to the hut, and left the fish on the porch. Rochana washed him and gave him sweets. After recounting the day's happenings, he suggested they go to court together.

When they paid respect to the king, the Negrito smiled foolishly and put down the fish.

"I'm afraid you will kill the Negrito because he has brought only two hundred fish," Rochana said. "We are poor and have no helper, not like your other daughters who have husbands with status. Have they come back yet? I suppose they've gotten many fish."

The king, wanting to hit Rochana, struck his cushion in anger.[26]

Meanwhile, the sons-in-law urged their servants to row the boat faster. Arriving at court and seeing the Negrito's fish, they sadly sat on the floor and bowed their heads.

"What has happened to your noses? Speak truthfully!" demanded the king.

"We left early in the morning, taking all our nets to where we expected fish," one of the men explained. "A globefish bit off our noses. We stayed out in the sun until we were black. We found a few fish in a pond, but there were never as few as this before. An evil spirit[27] must have been angry, for we got headaches and became drowsy."

The Negrito laughed and motioned to Rochana to look closely at the men with cut noses. Glad to see her sisters as uncomfortable as they had made her, she smiled with the Negrito.

Angrily her sisters pointed their fingers at her.

"Whom are you laughing at, Rochana? Our husbands are high-born. They can't fish like a Negrito. A man of the forest knows where to hunt for fish."

"Your husbands went to fish with servants. Mine went alone and didn't lose his nose. I know what happened, but I won't tell. Or do you really want me to tell?" Rochana teased.

A look from the Negrito made Rochana say no more. As she went out with her husband, Rochana spat lightly at her sisters.

"Who has closed your mouth? Tell us what happened," the sisters demanded.

When Rochana would not tell, they began to hit her and would not let her go. With gestures the Negrito tried to get them to give up Rochana. The sisters were afraid to touch the Negrito, but grimaced at him. Grabbing Rochana's hand, he got her to make the same face back at her sisters. Making fun of the men, the Negrito put a leaf on the end of his nose to keep off the flies.

The sons-in-law were so angry at the Negrito for

making fun of them in front of their wives that their eyes were green. One cursed him; another nudged him with his elbow. The Negrito waved his stick just above the ground so they could come no closer. One of the men shut his eyes and started to box with the Negrito, who then lifted his stick, throwing all the others off balance. The oldest went toward the Negrito, who then grabbed his hurt nose. The other men turned to flee.

When the sisters saw their husbands so afraid, they cursed Rochana:

"You don't speak against your husband, you just sit quietly. I'm an older sister, yet you revile me. You look down on some one older than yourself."

Rochana responded:

"In the beginning, who cursed whom? I can't make my husband put his hand in a bag. You don't act like a superior person, so I won't restrain my husband.[28] I'm sorry for your husband. He lost his nose-tip and then felt my husband's fist."

Queen Montha would hear no more:

"Why do you argue in front of your superiors? I've never seen such children. Will you kill each other?"

She told Rochana to take her husband out and asked the men to forbid their wives to speak so loudly.

When the king threatened to fight the Negrito himself, Rochana suggested they take leave of her father. She taught the Negrito to pay respect to the king in courtly fashion. He bowed low ten times. Before leaving he pointed again at the noses of the six men.

Infuriated, the king ordered his sons-in-law to hunt game.[29] When the soldiers arrived at the hut to deliver the king's order, Rochana was making clothes for the Negrito to wear to a Kathin festival.[30]

The next morning when the six men went to the forest seeking game, they found only tigers, bears, and cows. One suggested that they make an offering to the Lord of the Forest. Again they met Prince Sang, who demanded their ear-tips in exchange for game. When twenty deer came in answer to his prayer, Prince Sang gave each man only one, keeping the rest for himself. He did not take Rochana with him to court, for he felt he could fight if he need not fear for her safety.

When the six returned to the angry king, they explained that there must have been a bad spirit in the forest who hid the game. A knife which floated down out of the sky with no hand attached to it had cut off their ear-tips, they said.

When the Negrito saw the king was unhappy with his sons-in-law, he silently pointed to his own game, and to what the others had brought, counting the bodies. Then he pointed to a knife and to the neck of the eldest man.

"The Negrito must be an evil spirit, because he doesn't blink," said a son-in-law. "If he stays in the court, he will surely bring trouble."

King Samon believed him and ordered soldiers to chase the Negrito from the court. Laughing, the Negrito swung his stick. So fearful was the king that he fell from his couch. Queen Montha helped him up.

The Negrito took some water in his mouth and sprayed it out on the six. When they were quite wet, he took hold of one man by the ear, leading him around like a bullock. Paying respect to his mother-in-law, the Negrito indicated that he was going home.

When he got to the hut, he told Rochana all, and they were happy together.

The Polo Match

The heavenly throne of the thousand-eyed Indra became very hard.[31] Looking down through his magic eye, he saw the hardships Rochana suffered because Prince Sang would not take off his disguise. On orders from Indra, who descended to earth in his shimmering chariot, divinities transformed themselves into humans and as an army threatened the kingdom of Samon. With guns and loud cries they terrorized the countrymen, who picked up their few possessions, such as mats and betel containers, and prepared to flee, but found no sanctuary.[32]

Soldiers and courtiers went to tell the king. When his minor wives tried to rouse him, he slept on. Awakening, he asked Montha the meaning of a dream. "There is great danger," she replied with disgust, "and you want to tell your dream!"

When he realized that the city was surrounded, he talked on and on as one out of his mind. He asked the soldiers whether they should fight or flee, but felt he had no strength to fight. At last he ordered soldiers to close the doors on the four sides of the city wall and prepare hot pebbles and sand to hurl at any enemy who tried to climb the walls.

Indra ordered the deity Wisanukam[33] to take a note to King Samon proposing that he play polo[34] with the kingdom as the stake. Finding the doors of the kingdom closed, Wisanukam angrily kicked them in and went straight to the throne room. Montha caught Samon's hand as he tried to run away. Speaking as one higher than the king, Wisanukam read the message from his master:

"If you win, my kingdom will become a tributary of yours; if you lose I will take everything. If you don't play, I shall burn the kingdom."

Samon replied that his sons-in-law would play. As one drunk, he spoke of not being afraid, although he was terrified. Samon urged his sons-in-law to compete:

"Our enemies see that I am old so they propose this game. My eyes are not good, nor are my ears. I implore you to save the kingdom from falling into other hands."

Reluctantly they agreed. As the men bathed and dressed in preparation, their mirrors reflected their marred noses.

That afternoon, sitting on an elephant with the six sons-in-law on horses at either side, King Samon went to the polo field, crowded with people. Indra rode up to the men, asking in a loud voice:

"Are you the ones who will compete with me? Your faces are not like other people's. You've lost your ears and noses. Whose sons are you?"

When he was told they were the sons-in-law of King Samon, Indra began to play. Some of the men fell from

their horses: some struck in the wrong direction. One
pretended to smile at his wife. Some could not ride
at all.

Indra asked why no one returned his strike. Fearfully
they tried to play, but had no strength. They could
hardly lift their sticks from the ground, and gave up.
Indra came very close to the king and said:

"They have lost to me, but there is one more—the
husband of your youngest daughter. Do you want a
return match? If you don't, I shall take the kingdom."

"But he can't play polo; he's only a forest Negrito,"
Samon murmured, and wept.

"You should thank the challenger because he gives
another player a chance," encouraged Montha. "If the
Negrito is no longer angry at you, perhaps he will play
and win a tributary kingdom."

Taking heart, King Samon replied to his challenger:

"Wait. The Negrito can't speak or hear, but he's
strong. If this seventh can't win, I'll play no more. I will
lose. Wait until tomorrow."

When he asked Montha to extend his apologies to the
Negrito and urge him to compete, she thought it very
humorous that the king, who had been infuriated at the
Negrito, should have to send for him.

Rochana and the Negrito were cultivating vegetables
when Montha reached their hut. Happily Rochana ran
to her mother, inviting her to go into the house, and
urging her husband to pay respect.[35] He prepared betel
for Montha and put vegetables into a bag to give her.

"I'm bored with having you act stupid," Rochana said.

Montha explained why she had come to Rochana, asking her to urge her husband to compete. When Rochana told him she would die if he did not compete, the Negrito pitied her, but remembered how he had been treated. He turned his back to Montha, who urged, "If you are angry at Samon, think of me."

"The king said I was a bad spirit. No matter what you say, I think he wants to kill me. No one has pitied us, but now that I see you do, I thank you for coming," the Negrito ended with sarcasm.

"You can speak!" Montha exclaimed.

Saying he was very smart, she pleaded with him and Rochana to save the kingdom. When Rochana repeated that she would die unless he helped, he gave in.

Montha sent to the king for clothes when the Negrito said he had none. These he refused, and the king himself came with a second set which was also refused. Unseen by anyone except the Negrito, Wisanukam brought a suit from Indra. Delighted, Prince Sang took off the Negrito disguise and handed it to Rochana. As he came out of an inner room, Montha caught a glimpse of him and, thinking him a divinity, she paid respect. Rochana stopped her, explaining that the Negrito had thrown off a disguise. Montha called in the king, saying, "He's more beautiful than any other human being."

The king looked at his son-in-law and mused: "When I was young, I was handsome, but I could never compete with him. His skin is gold."

When asked whose son he was, Prince Sang paid respect to his father-in-law and said he was Sang Thong, the son of Yosawimon, and told his life story. A horse to his liking was all he asked to enter the competition. Though there were many in the royal stables, he requested a horse of mixed colors that he had seen in the fields.

When Prince Sang accepted the king's invitation to the palace, the six sons-in-law recognized him as the "Lord of the Forest." The older sisters fell in love with him. In their jealousy, they all began to criticize Rochana again. With no little relish she told the story of how the six had lost the tips of their ears and noses. The sons-in-law, not daring to deny her words, spoke of many other matters. King Samon ordered them to go and be the servants of Prince Sang.

When they all arrived on the polo field, Indra spoke to another divinity:

"Now I am satisfied. I can show his father-in-law that Prince Sang has power."

King Samon made an offering with a *bai si* [tiered structure containing food and sweetmeats; lit., "auspicious rice"] and a pig's head. He prayed and promised that if his son-in-law won, he would present *Inao* for nine days,[36] along with other entertainment. When Montha and King Samon blessed him, Prince Sang smiled with his wife. He took his polo stick and began to play.

When King Samon saw Prince Sang winning, he laughed. He fell, exhausted from cheering. Laughing as he drank, he nearly choked. Lighting a cigarette and throwing it away, he hit his wife's nose.

"Don't be afraid," he said. "Prince Sang will win."

He cursed his six sons-in-law, saying, "Looking after you is a waste of rice."

Then he called Rochana to come near him:

"Father can't see because he is old. Your eyes are still young. Show me where your husband is."

A cheer went up. Indra rode skyward from the field. Prince Sang rode after him. Everyone sat with upturned face and open mouth. The wise women of the court forbade the younger wives to make any noise. Indra pretended to lose. Passing Samon, he said:

"Your son-in-law is skillful. He competes and doesn't lose. If he had not done so, you would have lost everything. It is right that you give him the kingdom." Indra rode back up into the sky.

King Samon and Queen Montha embraced Prince Sang, and took him back to the court. As Samon had promised, *Inao* was given for nine days. There were *hun* [acting by doll puppets], *khon* [masked plays], and Chinese plays given by women.

Samon was busy making arrangements. He took Prince Sang to the ceremonial hall in a procession. When all arrived they sounded a gong and an old Brahman priest lit candles for the ceremony of *wian thian* [carrying or passing candles around one who is wished wellbeing].

King Samon and Queen Montha blessed Prince Sang and Rochana and gave them the kingdom.

🎋 ACT NINE

The Reunion

Indra then looked down on Chanthewi, still keeping herself alive on what she could gather in the forest. Bathing and dressing himself, Indra went to King Yosawimon by night. Carrying a stick as long as a sugar palm, he startled Yosawimon from sleep.

Threatened that, if he did not get up, Indra would beat him to death, Yosawimon responded that he would give all he had and become a priest, if he could keep but one woman to prepare his food. Explaining where the king's wife and son were, Indra ordered Yosawimon to get them within seven days or face death.

King Yosawimon thought how unhappy he had been without his queen or child, as he wept until morning. Then, neither bathing, dressing, nor eating, the king went to his soldiers, ordering them to make preparations for him to go to Chanthewi the next day.

When Chantha heard Yosawimon was going for Chanthewi, she was terrified. Trying to make the king ashamed so he would not go, she reproached him:

"You've forgotten what you once said. A king can't take back his words. You'll be like a stick put in soft earth that sways back and forth. If you spat on the ground and picked it up to swallow, would it not be hateful?"

152

Telling her she had no business being scornful of him, Yosawimon compared Chantha to a wounded ox who is afraid of a vulture hovering in the sky.

"You say that Indra came to you," Chantha persisted. "You're overcome by love-magic. You've drowned your son. Fish have eaten him and only his bones are left. Are you going to follow him into the water?"

Angry at Chantha for her sarcasm and implication that he lied, the king called her "evil as a poisonous snake" and beat her.

Arriving at a forest camp, Yosawimon sent soldiers to find Chanthewi. When they came back, having found her thin and tired, the king took her favorite maids with him. As he neared the place where Chanthewi stayed, she saw him and hid with the old couple in the cottage. Following her, the king tried to comfort her as he explained that Indra had told him where they could find their son.

Overjoyed that their son was alive, she was no longer angry with the king. She agreed to go with him, saying:

"When I suffered hardships I depended on old grandmother and grandfather. Graciously repay their kindness."

The king urged the old people to come out of hiding. Heads lowered and trembling with fear, they came. He took them to his forest camp and gave them a betel container, money, clothes, and servants. He bestowed a title upon the old man, putting him above all other people in the countryside. The old people called their new servants to take their rewards home. So proud were they, that they failed to notice anyone who now respectfully greeted them along the way.[37]

The king climbed onto an elephant, with Chanthewi enclosed in a chariot. To the sound of gong, conch, and horn they set out for the kingdom of Samon. When they neared the walls of Samon, Yosawimon suggested that Chanthewi go in first, fearing that Prince Sang might feel great resentment toward him.

Chanthewi replied:

"What sort of daring person are you to have your wife go first? Why are you afraid of your son more than of a tiger in the forest? Our child has inherited a king-dom: to hurt his father and mother would be against custom. Don't be afraid. I'll be the one to speak."

They decided to disguise themselves as poor country-folk before entering the city.[38] The tradeswomen noticed how much Yosawimon looked like the son-in-law of Samon. Observing the gentle ways of Chanthewi, they thought she was a woman who had once had status and riches but had fallen on hard times. Using family names of respect, they called to the couple to look at their wares or stop to chew some betel. Yosawimon pretended to look at things as one who had never seen their like. They bargained, trying to strike good prices. Chan-thewi urged her husband away from a shop, saying:

"It isn't proper for one of your age to use cloth like that. Let's buy toys for our grandchildren instead."

At dusk, they stopped at a *sala* [open pavilion] where travelers might stay. "At night a guard will come to inspect," Yosawimon reminded Chanthewi. "If we're walking about, it will not go well with us." They lit a fire and slept.

Meanwhile Prince Sang slept fitfully as his thoughts turned to his mother. Rochana sympathized with his unhappiness. The next day he ordered his soldiers to prepare the procession for an inspection of the city.

When King Yosawimon heard the sound of the procession, he and Chanthewi went out to watch. "This one, is he our son?" asked Yosawimon. Chanthewi stared and said that, though his body was like Prince Sang's, his golden skin was not as she remembered it. Forgetting themselves, they went close to the procession and were driven back by soldiers.

When the procession had passed, Yosawimon remarked to Chanthewi:

"The great man looked at you much more than at me. There was sadness in his eyes."

Chanthewi suggested that the king stay with the gatekeeper while she went to get work in the palace kitchen. One day she made a vegetable curry, carving each of seven vegetables to represent an incident in the life of Prince Sang, from the time she herself had borne a shell to the time the prince was thrown into the water.

When he dipped into the curry and picked up a piece, Prince Sang was amazed, and he wondered. Picking them out one by one, he put them in a row and found the story of the conch shell. Crying, he asked that the person who had made the curry be sent to him.

The servants wondered when they saw Prince Sang crying. They frightened the cooks, saying, "He must be very angry: the one who made the curry should go to him at once." Chanthewi soothed them "Never mind," she said, "If it is anyone's fault, I will take all the blame."

When he saw his mother, Prince Sang ran to embrace her feet and fainted. Both his mother and Rochana fainted too. Servants ran to tell King Samon and Montha, who went crying into the room of their son-in-law. When a doctor had brought the three back to consciousness with massage and snuff, Prince Sang explained everything to Samon and Montha.

Chanthewi asked Prince Sang not to be angry with his father. He replied:

"Father punished me, but I am not angry. It was the result of my bad deeds from a former life. I know it was karma that parted us. But now I want to see him, too."

Chanthewi explained that he was a servant of the gatekeeper, making bamboo rice-containers. Together they all went to the city gate. Prince Sang embraced Yosawimon's right leg, while Chanthewi embraced his left. Returning his son's embrace, Yosawimon cried.

"I have done wrong," he said, "I punished you. But you didn't die because you had much merit. Come back with me and I shall give you the kingdom."

Assuring his father that he bore no ill feeling toward him, Prince Sang and the others paid respect to King Yosawimon. Upon Samon's insistence that it was not right for them to talk by the side of the road, they all returned to the palace, where they drank tea as Rochana fanned them.

While Yosawimon and Chanthewi stayed with Prince Sang, Rochana looked after them. When Prince Sang was to go back to the kingdom of Yosawimon to keep the promise to Indra, he asked Rochana if she wished to go with him or stay. "Wherever you go I shall go until I die," Rochana answered.

King Samon asked that, when he died, Prince Sang would take the responsibility for his cremation. Montha embraced Rochana, telling her to do as her husband, Yosawimon, and Chanthewi wished. "If Prince Sang is angry," she counseled, "don't return his anger."

As the soldiers were preparing for the procession back to the kingdom of Yosawimon, Samon said:

"When you have all left we shall be very lonely. When Prince Sang has met Indra, let the two come back here. I don't think of him as a son-in-law but as a son of my own. Please look after my daughter."

Yosawimon replied:

"Don't worry. We love Rochana as our daughter. We will take them now but then have them return. In the meantime may you rule with happiness and well-being."

Samon and Montha accompanied them to where the elephants waited. King Yosawimon and Prince Sang led on elephantback; Chanthewi and Rochana followed in a gilded chariot with their maids behind them. Slowly, to the sound of horn and gong, the procession departed.

Notes

1. The concept of the interaction of a great and a little tradition is from Robert Redfield, "The Social Organization of Tradition," chapter 3 of his *Peasant Society and Culture* (Chicago: University of Chicago Press, 1956).

2. The *Panyasachatok* [Fifty Birth-Stories], 2 vols. (Bangkok: National Library, 1956) is a Thai translation of the *Paññāsa Jātaka*. It actually contains fifty stories with eleven more appended to them. The story corresponding to that of Sang Thong is one of these eleven. Prince Damrong, however, in his introduction to this volume, makes no distinction between the writing of the first fifty stories and that of the eleven additional ones. Manuscripts of the *Paññāsa Jātaka* found in Laos and Cambodia contain the "Suvarna-Sankha-Jātaka" as no. 6 in the Laotian version and no. 41 in the Cambodian, according to Louis Finot ("Recherches sur la littérature laotienne," *Bulletin de l'École Française d'Extrême-Orient* 17, no. 5 [1917]: 48). Thus it would seem that the distinction between the fifty and the eleven has not been significant.

159

3. Damrong Rachanuphap (Prince), "Introduction," *Panyasachatok* 1: iii.

4. The *Nipātā Jātaka* is part of the *Sutta-Pitaka,* one of the three main sections of the Buddhist *Tripitaka.*

5. Damrong Rachanuphap (Prince), "Introduction," *Panyasachatok* 1: iii–iv.

6. The general theme of a part of "Suvarna-Sankha-Jātaka," however, seems to be taken from a section of the Pali canon called *Cariyā-Pitaka* (*Panyasachatok* 2: 226 fn).

7. I am indebted to Visudh Busyakul, professor of Sanskrit at Chulalongkorn University, Bangkok, for his search for evidence of the Sang Thong story in the *Divyāvadāna* and *Mahāvastu.*

8. Dhanit Yupho, *The Khon and Lakon* (Bangkok: Department of Fine Arts, 1963), p. 123.

9. Ariane Macdonald, "La Naissance du monde au Tibet," in *La Naissance du monde,* Sources orientales, vol. 1 (Paris: Éditions du Seuil, 1959), p. 428.

10. Mircea Eliade, *Myth and Reality,* trans. Willard R. Trask (New York: Harper and Row, 1963), p. 22. Reprinted by permission of the publisher.

11. Actually David Snellgrove and Hugh Richardson, authors of *A Cultural History of Tibet* (New York: Frederick A. Praeger, 1968), in which the bards' song appears (p. 57), do not clearly indicate its date. For other similar material, however, they indicate as their source the Tibetan documents believed to have been sealed in the Tun-huang caves in the 8th or 9th century.

12. Dwijendra Nath Neogi, *Sacred Tales of India* (London: Macmillan and Co., 1961), pp. 72–79.

13. Henry Parker, trans., *Village Folk-Tales of Ceylon,* 3 vols. (London: Luzac and Co., 1914), 3: 152–54.

14. Opinion expressed at a meeting of the History of Thai Art Study Group, directed by Victor Kennedy, in Bangkok, Thailand, March 1969.

15. Dhanit, *The Khon and Lakon,* p. 123.

16. Simon de La Loubère, *Royaume de Siam,* chap. 6 (cited in René Nicholas, "Le Lakhon Nora ou lakhon chatri et les origines du théâtre classique siamois," *Journal of the Siam Society* 18, no. 2 [1924]: 86).

17. Ibid., p. 88. Although Nicholas thought that La Loubère's description was of *lakhon nok,* it might well have been descriptive of *lakhon chatri,* an earlier form of Thai country dance-drama which was similar to the Indian dance-drama. *Lakhon chatri* evolved naturally into *lakhon nok* with the addition of more stories, players, musical instruments, and song patterns, and the inclusion of humorous material. Although we may for the sake of clarity put labels on forms which in their own time were unnamed, these labels often prove difficult to apply as one form blends with another in the course of time. It is unfortunate that La Loubère did not name the play, since "Manora" was the only story played as *lakhon chatri.* "Sang Thong" was added to country drama, along with other stories, as the *lakhon nok* style developed.

18. Montri Tramod, *Kanlalen Khawng Thai* [Thai Entertainment] (Bangkok: Phrachan, 1954), pp. 8–9.

19. *Bot Lakhon Khrang Krung Kao Rueang Nang Manora Lae Sang Thong* [Scripts for Dance-Dramas from Former Times: *Manora* and *Sang Thong*] (Bangkok: National Library, 1955), pp. 60–130.

20. Damrong Rachanuphap (Prince), *Phrarachaphong-sawadan Krung Ratanakosin Ratchakan II* [History of the Reign of Rama II] (Bangkok: Samnakngan Siam Bannagan, 1929), p. 452.

21. Damrong Rachanuphap (Prince), "Introduction," Phra Putthaloetla [King Rama II], *Bot Lakhon Nok Ruam 6 Rueang: Phrarachaniphon Ratchakan II* [Scripts for Six Dance-Dramas in the Style of *Lakhon Nok,* by King Rama II et al.] (Bangkok: National Library, 1958), pp. ii–iii. Other Thai scholars of history and drama think Rama II wanted to try his hand at writing plebian-style drama for the populace.

22. Damrong Rachanuphap (Prince), *Phrarachaphongsawadan Krung Ratanakosin Ratchakan II,* p. 464.

23. Ayumongol Sonakul, "Understanding the Negrito: King Chulalongkorn's Efforts Result in a Play," *Standard: Bangkok Magazine,* October 27, 1968, pp. 12–14.

24. Interview with Dhanit Yupho, Bangkok, April, 1969.

25. Jeanne Cuisinier, *Danses cambodgiennes* (Hanoi: Imprimerie d'Extrême-Orient, 1930), pp. 93–95.

26. James R. Brandon, *Theatre in Southeast Asia* (Cambridge: Harvard University Press, 1967), p. 27.

27. Prince Damrong wrote of this burning in his introduction to the Thai *Panyasachatok,* p. iv. Phya Anuman Rajadhon also spoke of the event in an interview (Bangkok, September 20, 1968).

28. This Burmese volume was published by the Hanthawaddy Press with the title *Zimme Pannāsa.* Louis Finot writes that it was "without doubt from a manuscript provided from Chiang Mai." (Zimme was the Burmese name for Chiang Mai.) Thus it would seem either that the burning of a *Pannāsa Jātaka* manuscript by a Burmese king did not destroy all copies extant in Burma by that time or that there was later intercourse between Chiang Mai and Rangoon.

29. Margaret Mead, "The Study of National Character,"

in *The Policy Sciences,* ed. Daniel Lerner and Harold D. Lasswell (Stanford: Stanford University Press, 1951), p. 74.

ACT ONE

1. "I" refers to the narrator, who in National Theater productions sings the first line followed by a chorus singing the second.

2. "Yosawimon" is from the Pali *yaso* (renowned) and *vimala* (pure, without blemish). See Jean Drans, *Histoire de Nang Manora et histoire de Sang Thong* (Tokyo: Presses Salesiennes, 1947). Many Thai names have their origin in Pali.

3. Traditionally, the king has gone around the city periodically to see that all was well. In recent practice the king makes such an inspection only after the inauguration ceremony. The present King repeated the tradition on his thirty-sixth birthday.

4. In literature Thais use many honorific phrases designating the king: "He Who Sits in the Lap of the Nāga"; "Ruler of the World"; "Ruler of the Sky": "Holder of the Ten Virtues"; "Powerful One"; "Bearer of the Discus"; "Winner of Victory"; "Bearer of the Truth."

5. To be unable to enjoy bathing signifies for Thais one of the greatest discomforts a person can experience. As one of the necessities and pleasures of life where the air is so often heavy with tropical heat, bathing is important in the lives of both city and country Thais. Village people will often carry water long distances in order to bathe. A common afternoon greeting between them is "Have you bathed yet?" Not bathing, therefore, expresses the king's disturbed feelings here and in other parts of the play.

6. The terms *heart* and *eyes* indicate that the person is as precious to the speaker as those vital organs of the body.

Although numerous words exist in written Thai for the loved one, neither these nor others are used when men and women or parents and children speak to each other.

7.   The king refers to himself as *phi*—the same term village Thais use when a husband refers to himself or his wife refers to him. It is also the term that is used for any older sibling. It implies the whole *phi-nawng* (older-younger) relationship so important in Thailand; for the person who is *phi* expects to give protection and sustenance, while the one who is *nawng* expects to respond with obedience and loyalty.

8.   Merit (*bun*) is the accumulation of good deeds from one's past and present existences. It can be built up by observing the Buddhist precepts (see note 10, below), feeding the priests and serving them in other ways, and by helping one's fellow men. (A taxi driver recently explained to me that the merit one builds up for his future life is just like the money one puts into the bank to make him more comfortable in the future years of his present life.)

9.   Since the *thewa, thewada,* or *thep* are in some ways like angels in the Christian tradition and in some ways like gods in the Greek sense, but unlike either in some respects, the more neutral terms *divinity* or *deity* seem the best translations. Like angels, they are the spirits of virtuous people who have died. In Thai terms they have much merit. Like the angels of Dante's world, they are ranked, living in stratified realms of heaven. One of these realms is called Dawadueng. These deities are responsive to the prayers of people on earth, but are not as powerful as gods in the Greek sense, even within a limited sphere. Unlike Christian angels and Greek gods, all *thewa,* except those in the highest realm, must return to earth to live again as human beings. Those in the highest realm bear similarities to Brahman gods.

10. The five vows or precepts which many Thais take each priest's day (rather like Sunday but occurring four times each lunar month) are: (1) not to kill animals; (2) not to steal; (3) not to take the wife or children of another; (4) not to lie; and (5) not to drink strong drink.

11. Until the reign of Rama VI, who ascended the throne in 1910, Thai kings maintained harems. One woman was considered queen, though there were countless lesser wives and their maids.

12. The status of the person about to act is often shown by the first word of a verse. Translated as "then," "at that time," or "meanwhile," *muea nan* indicates that a person of high status is about to act and *bat nan* means that someone of low status will act. Occasionally *muea nan* is used if a person of low status is about to do something very important.

13. The sentence "I shall depend upon you and give my life to you" expresses the ideal reciprocal relationship, in which the person of lesser status gives his or her life in respectful, obedient service and in return is able to depend upon the person of higher status.

14. These *thao* (a courtly title) *nang* (women) called upon by Yosawimon were elderly women in the court who, though not in the position of wives of the king, had great influence because of their knowledge of court procedures and ceremonies. Each *thao nang* was responsible for a different aspect of court life, e.g., arranging flowers or laying out proper clothes.

15. The phrase used here, *bucha banakan,* implies an offering or gift to a person of high status, in this case the deities. It is interesting that the word for the gift (*banakan*) denotes the status of the receiver.

16. The meaning seems deliberately and suggestively

ambiguous. Perhaps the maids, as well as the king's wives, took turns making offerings to the deities or sleeping protectively around the king, as was the custom, or perhaps sleeping with him. Quite possibly, they took turns at all three. Pragmatically, a Thai often uses both natural and supernatural means to achieve a desired result.

17.   *Hen kae na* (literally, to "pay attention to face") means to care about or respect someone because of his or her high position. Thus when King Yosawimon asserts that he does not care (*mai hen kae na*) about the usual hierarchical statuses of his wives, he is expressing his overwhelming desire for a son, which outweighs the usual Thai value of status respect.

18.   King Yosawimon requires his wives to *bon* (pray, or ask with conditions) *ban* (untranslatable word added for pleasing sound). Implicit in the term *bon ban* is the idea that the women are both to pray for a son and to promise gifts to the deities if this specific desire is fulfilled. Thus reciprocity, which is so important in Thai human relations, is evident here in relations with the deities.

19.   King Yosawimon tries in various ways to ensure the birth of a son. To *buang suang* (pay homage, or propitiate) may include a petition but does not involve a promise as does *bon ban*. Food, flowers, and incense are offered unconditionally at the time of *buang suang*. Such a *buang suang* ceremony is frequently repeated by large groups of people in Thailand today. Recently at Ayutthaya there was a large gathering of people to *buang suang winyan Phra Naresuan*. The immortal spirit of Phra Naresuan, a beloved king (r. A.D. 1590–1605), was thus presented with gifts. Often the *phra sayam thewa thirat* (deity protecting Thailand) is honored by those who come together to *buang suang*.

20. To Thais the *dechasomphan* (royal power) is thought to be a force within the king himself and yet beyond the person of any one king. Thais today explain that they personally feel that they are able to accomplish difficult tasks and fulfill their needs both by the power of their own merit and by the power of the king.

21. Priests are mentioned separately because of the special position of respect in which a Buddhist priest is held.

22. The responsibility of the king for ensuring the happiness of his people is often repeated in *Sang Thong,* as in Thai tradition. When King Samon and King Yosawimon himself become humorous figures in later acts in the style of *lakhon nok,* there is the feeling that they are fallible human beings falling short of the ideal.

23. King Yosawimon and his wife call on the *phra suea meuang* (Lord of the Land; literally, "venerable inhuman of the kingdom"), who is a special deity protecting a given country.

24. The ten virtues, which were expounded in the Buddhist Tammasat and have been held as the ideal for Thai kings, are: (1) charity; (2) moral living according to the known code; (3) support for religion; (4) honesty; (5) compassion; (6) freedom from wrongful ambition; (7) freedom from thoughts of revenge; (8) love for the people as their father; (9) moderation in punishment; (10) constant care of the people's welfare and happiness (Chula Chakrabongse [Prince], *Lords of Life: A History of the Kings of Thailand* [London: Redman, 1960], p. 85).

25. The *winyan* (spirit) which survives after a person or deity ends the current life, goes on from existence to existence. It enters the womb of a mother at the moment of conception.

26. In Thailand dreams are very carefully remembered and interpreted as omens.

27. Fortune-tellers are reputed to be reluctant to disclose future misfortune. This is an aspect of a more general Thai value, that of keeping situations seemingly comfortable and happy.

28. Since the right hand is considered more important than the left, the most important queen was called the Queen at the Right.

29. "Chanthewi" is from the Pali *cando* (moon) and *devī* (queen, goddess).

30. In accord with the traditional Thai belief that like can cause like, beautiful people around the mother can affect the appearance of the unborn child.

31. The king, when called *phra chakri* (Bearer of the Discus), is vaguely identified with a divinity, Phra Narai, who carries a discus and can split himself into parts which then become human beings. The present dynasty is called the Chakri dynasty.

32. The traditional Thai relationship between the king (or the queen) and servants is that between parents and children.

33. The literal translation is "into the house," but many Thais understand this as "up on the porch," since this is the area where guests were usually received in traditional Thai houses, as in village houses today.

34. The traditional Thai greeting, in its varied forms, is called a *wai*. Phya Anuman Rajadhon writes that a particularly beautiful form of the *wai* may be seen on the stage in Thai *lakhon*. In the performance of this gesture the Thai actor or actress, before lifting his or her hands, brings the palms together "with the finger tips drawn slightly to each

other, so as to form a conventional shape of a budding lotus as usually offered in worship to a monk or a Buddha image" (*Essays on Thai Folklore* [Bangkok: Social Science Press of Thailand, 1968], p. 179). When a man or woman "greets," "bids farewell," or "pays respect" to another in the present translation, it is usually with a *wai*.

35. The nomenclature of family relationship is often extended outside the family, sometimes with feelings of love, respect, and loyalty appropriate to those within it, but sometimes simply with recognition of the age group of one or another family member.

36. The *chang* was a measure of Thai money in former times. It was equal to eighty *baht*, a *baht* today being equal to five American cents. In the days when the *chang* was used, five *chang* would have been a large amount of money.

37. Like the reckoning of age, for which the beginning rather than the end of the first year is called "one," the reckoning of pregnancy counts the beginning of the first month, rather than the end, as "one."

38. In Thai folk-belief, the stomach is divided into two parts, one of which holds the developing child. There is no vocabulary differentiation, such as that indicated by the English words *stomach* and *womb*.

39. *Kam* is a term for which it is impossible to give a simple literal translation or even explanation, except perhaps "one's deeds, and their consequences in another lifetime." *Kam* is pivotal in the Thai view of life and thus would be enough to explain all of Chanthewi's misfortunes. The Thai concept of *kam* is like the Indian idea of karma. Karma, however, is a neutral word referring to the store of both good and bad deeds an individual builds up through his successive existences and the inevitable influences these have.

Kam, in popular Thai thought, is generally considered to be the bad deeds one has done in a former existence and the consequences of these deeds. When someone is unhappy, sick, or poor, he and others interpret this to be the result of his *kam.* Sometimes it is a comforting belief, since one may feel his misfortune is no fault of his own in the present existence and that his present suffering will end when he has expiated the consequences of his misdeeds of a former life.

40.   The idea of *kam* may also be a source of embarrassment and shame, because a misfortune in the present life may be interpreted by others as an indication of one's sins in a former life.

41.   Beating the breast, as Chanthewi does here, and also hitting one's head are gestures commonly seen in Thai *lakhon.* They are Thai women's expressions, in their own homes, of feelings of despair in impossible situations.

42.   The astrologer would have had to wait outside, since no man, except the king, could enter the women's court.

43.   In the past, a woman lay on a bamboo bed close to a charcoal fire after childbirth. Bangkok women, following the example of a brave queen of King Chulalongkorn, broke this tradition, but the custom is still practiced in villages. Thai women commonly explain that the fire dries the womb and brings it back to normalcy. Jane Hanks feels after research in village Thailand that a woman is thought to become "ritually mature through the fire-rest experience" just as a man does through entry, for a period, into the priesthood (*Maternity and Its Rituals in Bang Chan,* Southeast Asia Program Data Paper no. 51 [Ithaca, N.Y.: Cornell University, 1962], pp. 73–77).

44.   The concept of a god of death, Yama, is Indian rather than Thai. Since the Indian god is not thought of as burning

kingdoms, his figure may here be combined with the Thai memory of the sacking of their former capital, Ayutthaya, by the Burmese.

45. In this line the queen is called the king's *ming khwan*. In Thai a father and mother are said to be the *ming khwan* (protectors of the spirits) of their children. Husbands and wives are each other's *ming khwan*. As for the king and queen, they are both the *ming khwan* (protectors of the spirits) of the people.

46. The astrologer has called the queen a *kali*. If misfortune comes to a group of people, it may be caused spiritually by one among them, often a newcomer, according to Thai folk-belief. Although this belief is apparently less prevalent than it was in the past, I have recently heard that sickness causing the death of many pigs was thought by farmers to be caused by the presence of a *kali* in a village.

The Indian Hindu goddess Kālī is a bearer of evil, but only to those who are themselves evil. In a *jātaka* tale of the Theravada Buddhists, Kālī appears as the goddess of ill-luck. The Thai belief accounting for the loss of pigs suggests that handling of the theme of misfortune in both Indian Buddhist and Thai folk-traditions may have been responsible for the transformation of the Indian Hindu goddess Kālī, bearer of evil to evildoers, into a Thai *kali* who is feared, in *Sang Thong,* as a human bearer of evil to all. (The Buddhist tale referred to is "Sirikalākanni-Jātaka," in E.B. Cowell, ed., *"The Jātaka": or Stories of Buddha's Former Births,* 6 vols. [Cambridge University Press, 1895–1907], 3: 163–68.)

47. Although the king accepts the idea that his wife's deeds of a former life have caused the present misfortune, with the possibility of more to come, he does not feel that in her present life-span she is in any way guilty.

48.   The king's question, "Who could separate calmly?" recognizes the Thai ethic of controlling oneself and the expression of one's feelings.

49.   The king seems to recognize two levels of "reason": the reason of the comprehensive moral logic of *kam* and the lack of reason in their current lives.

50.   When the *khwan* (spirit, feeling of well-being) leaves the body, as it has here left Chanthewi's body, the person may become very ill or die, according to prevalent Thai belief.

51.   The king's "don't make too much of this" is, literally, "don't diagnose that you will die." The frequently used Thai saying *Ya ti tua kawn khai* (Don't diagnose the body's illness as grave before there is fever) expresses the same Thai value of minimizing trouble.

52.   *Wen kam* or *wera kam,* as it is used in the line "Because the turn of fate is that way," is a common Thai expression, which means that the time has come or is soon to come when one must inevitably experience the appropriate consequences, usually bad, of what one has done in a former life.

53.   The king is ashamed of his tears.

54.   Chantha's treachery in saying that the king's men should pay the queen no respect *(ya wai na)* is especially serious in a country where respect for people in high places, particularly royalty, is very great.

55.   Literally, the people are called *phrai* (servants, common people) *fa* (heaven). The king is here thought of as the ruler of all earth and heaven, with people, under normal conditions, acting as his willing servants.

56.   *Khap chai,* the phrase describing the king's constraint, expresses a very uncomfortable feeling of being hemmed in by the demands of others. There is a familiar Thai say-

ing: *Khap thi yu dai; khap chai yu yak* (To live in a small
place is easy, but to live hemmed in by demands is difficult).

57. *Bai buean* (speaking diplomatically) is literally *bai*
(turning the head) *beuan* (turning the body), or, when used
together, "speaking deviously." *Bai beuan* has positive meaning because of the value Thais place on easing a situation and
making people feel better. The phrase, applied here to Yosawimon's manner of speech to Chanthewi, is difficult to translate
into English because of the value Westerners place on direct-
ness of speech.

58. Explanations of the working of *kam* often involve
reconstruction of presumed situations in which one may have
erred in a past life and which bear a resemblance to the
consequences one is suffering in one's present existence.

59. *Kam* is inevitable, like an account that must be paid.

60. The king calls his wife *nawng ruam hawng* (younger
one who shares the same room). In Thai there are also
nawng ruam tawng (younger brothers and sisters born from the
same stomach [mother]) and *nawng ruam lok* (younger friends
of the same world [community]).

61. As one goes through life and accumulates good deeds,
these become his *bun* which result in good circumstances
later. *Bun* and *bap* (or *kam*) cannot cancel each other. They
are separate accounts, each of which must be paid in turn.

62. The play is from a period when there were no doors
in the palace, only curtains. The curtains the king closes here
were the same sort, ironically, that were pulled apart on
special occasions to show his radiant presence. This, along
with the description of the sparkling room, adds to the pathos
of the king's misery.

63. The phrase translated "overwhelmed" here is,
literally, "angered and made sorrowful a hundred thousand

fold." A number is placed on feelings, although Thais are generally less apt than Westerners to use numbers for measuring distance and time.

64. The king is called *phan pi* (thousand years), implying he holds all the wisdom, dignity, and respect this age might bring.

65. The queen calls herself *nawng kaow*, literally, "younger" and "precious."

66. The queen asks for a seven-day delay because after childbirth a woman must lie by the fire for a minimum of seven days. Any odd number of days beyond this amount (e.g., nine, eleven, thirteen), is thought by some village women to be of even greater benefit.

67. When a woman is pregnant, the elements of fire, wind, earth, and water are not in normal proportion in her body.

68. The poetic pathos of this scene is increased if one visualizes the beautiful, intricately designed gold of the long, wide bench, perhaps about two feet from the floor, on which Chanthewi laments, and on which a king and queen would often sit together.

69. The sort of sarcasm found in this remark on Chantha's "goodness" is frequent in Thai writing and speaking.

70. The king is here referred to as *phumin pinglao* (Ruler of the Land, Top Knot of the Head). Since the second term is used to refer to the very top of the head, it is used here to denote the king who is at the head of his people.

71. Poignantly, with no apparent knowledge of the contents of the shell, the queen thinks of it as her son since she gave it birth.

72. "I shall no longer serve you" is, literally, "I cannot lie under your feet." The queen's feeling is one of sorrow.

Her relationship of serving her husband the king has seemed right to her. (When one would speak of the face or head of a common person, one speaks of the foot of the king, because even this low part of the body is high when it is part of the king's person.)

73. If one gets the pardon of another, one may not have to suffer in another life for any wrong to that person. In this way an individual may hope to influence karma. It is common, at the time of death, for family, friends, and acquaintances of the deceased to pour water on his hands as they offer forgiveness for any wrong he may have done to them and ask pardon for any wrong they may have committed, knowingly or unknowingly, against him.

74. "Long life" here is, literally, "ten thousand years." An exaggerated number is used for something important.

75. "They," here, refers to Chantha and her followers. Pronoun references in Thai often seem unclear to Westerners. When placing absolute blame might make the situation more difficult, as it might here, language construction serves the Thai value of minimizing the face-to-face conflict in a situation.

76. The queen infers from her loss of status that the store of merit in her karmic account has diminished. One who has status is thought to have merit from a past life. Therefore it is right that Chanthewi should be able to order others. However, if she loses this status, it would be wrong for her to be served by others and could only add to her misfortune for still another life.

77. In Thai folklore and drama, the *kinnon* or *kinnari* (bird-maiden) to which Chanthewi is here compared is half beautiful woman, half bird, living in the mountain forests far away from humans. This is a transformation of the Hindu

mythological concept of *kinnaras,* "beings with the form of a man and the head of a horse. They are celestial choristers and musicians, dwelling on the paradise of Kuvera on Kailāsa" (John Dowson, *A Classical Dictionary of Hindu Mythology and Religion, Geography, History, and Literature.* 7th ed. [London: Routledge and Kegan Paul, 1950], p. 158).

In the *Mahāvastu,* which contains birth-stories of the Mahayana Buddhists, there is a story about a girl with a beautiful face, figure, and voice, Manoharā, who is a *kinnari.*

The story of Manora, the half–beautiful woman, half-bird figure, exists in other parts of Southeast Asia; hence it seems that both Buddhist beliefs and folk beliefs were responsible for transforming the Indian Hindu image.

78.   Thai women occasionally *khawn* (narrow the eyes and tighten the mouth to a hard line) to express their displeasure, in the type of glance described here. This expression, incongruent with the ideal values of self-control and smooth interpersonal relationships, normally is revealed only in intimate, private situations.

79.   Expressed in Chanthewi's reproach to the shell is the utter wrongness of a situation where the Thai value of reciprocity in human relationships is not fulfilled. Although reciprocity exists in Western relationships, the expectation of it is not as open as it is for Thais. Thus, the mother says, "I have looked after you *so that* you could be a friend."

80.   Rural people, like those Chanthewi lives with, commonly prepared flour for steamed, fried, or roasted cakes by drying rice on large trays made of woven bamboo strips.

81.   Chanthewi's carrying stick is probably like those carried on one shoulder with a basket suspended from each end, used for carrying a variety of things in rural Thailand.

In the city it is less common but still used by hawkers going through the lanes selling their wares.

82. The *thepthai* (spirit living in the trees) seems to be a link between the Buddhist-Brahman idea of heavenly deities and the animistic belief in malevolent spirits who often inhabit the trees. These *thepthai* are unseen beings who have somewhat less merit than the heavenly deities; but, like the good tree-spirit who pities Chanthewi, they do have the power to look after people who pass or those who live near the trees the *thepthai* inhabit. If a person has a feeling of well-being when he passes a certain tree, he knows there is a good spirit in it.

83. This is a pair of common sayings describing those who have much merit. The importance of not being carried away by a current or burned by a fire is especially felt in a country of many rivers and canals and of open cooking fires.

84. The term *din fa badan*, referring to the three worlds of earth, heaven, and land-water below the earth, corresponds in part to the Brahman belief in three worlds: *svarga* (heaven), *bhumi* (earth), and *pātāla* (hell), which together are known as Tribhuvana or Triloka. Although Thai Buddhist temple walls often picture the pains of hell, cosmology expressed in literature presents the land-water area below the earth as a neutral region. This cosmological concept entered the Thai literary tradition in the period of the Kingdom of Sukhothai (A.D. 1275–1350). "During the reign of King Litai, enlightened ruler of the Kingdom of Sukhodaya [Sukhothai], and very likely under his own authorship, the first great work of Thai literature appeared: *Traibhumikatha* [The Story of the Three Worlds], a treatise on Buddhist cosmology, written A.D. 1345" (Prem Purachatra [Prince], "Thai Literature: A Brief Survey," mimeographed [Seventh

lecture in a series organized by the Thailand Council of the Asia Society, New York, N.Y., June, 1963]).

85.   People who are happy together are called *khu sang, khu som* (literally, "couple built, couple fit"). In a former life, it is explained, they made merit together and wished to live together in a future existence. Urban and rural people, both young and old, explain that a man and woman who have made merit together in a former life and who wish to live together in a future existence are destined for this happiness. Thus it is implied that Rochana and Prince Sang were together in a former existence and were destined to be a pair in the future.

86.   The following two verses (concerning Prince Sang's awareness of how his mother has loved and protected him and his effort to chase away the wild chickens and prepare food for her) are taught in the fourth grade of many Thai schools to instill in children from an early age a sense of the right sort of mutually helpful relationship between parents and children.

87.   The Thai word for *then* used here is different from the one used in other verses, and the entire verse moves faster than most. For this reason the word does not appear on a separate line here. (See note 12, above.)

88.   This simile is common in Thai and Indian literature. In comparing someone's face to the moon, one thinks of the brightness of the moon, rather than of its shape.

89.   Chanthewi mistakes her son for a *phi ruean* (the spirit of the first owner of a house) who stays in the house giving protection, though sometimes also trouble, to its inhabitants.

90.   The phrase used here to describe Prince Sang's feelings, *fai lon,* means to be held up to a fire like a piece of wax someone is trying to soften in order to mold it. It expresses

the anxiety one feels when a situation affecting him is beyond his control.

91.   Though theoretically *khraw* (luck), like *kam* (consequences of actions in a past life), is a neutral term, it is
usually thought of as bad. Present good fortune signifies to
the queen, as it often does to Thai villagers, that her *khraw*
and her *kam* are both finished.

92.   The old people feel that seeing such a beautiful crea-
ture is a reward for their past good deeds, which therefore
must have existed.

93.   *Sang* (to build) is used. Although Buddhism does not
posit a creator, Brahmanism, which is inseparable from
Buddhism in the thoughts of most Thais, posits that all things
were and are built by Brahma.

ACT TWO

1.   This saying about the lizard who received gold refers
to a folk tale well known in Thailand. A king, greatly im-
pressed with the respect shown by a lizard who bobbed its
head, gave gold to a gardener to feed it. One day when the
gardener could find no food, he hung two coins around the
lizard's neck instead. Proudly the lizard went about showing
its gold and saying that it received food from the king.
When the king later passed the gate, the proud lizard haugh-
tily showed no respect. The king ordered the gardener to
feed it no longer.

2.   *Phi hong* is the dead body, or ghost, of a person who
has died by violence; *phi phrai,* of a woman who has died
in childbirth. Both have strong powers for making love-
magic, as the old woman's use of the two skulls indicates here.

3.   Betel, which is a mixture of the fruit from an arreca
palm and a little lime wrapped in the leaves of a pepper plant,

was commonly chewed throughout Thailand until recent years. It is still enjoyed by old people in the countryside.

4. Village Thais commonly use Chantha's threat, or similar ones, to make their children behave.

5. The Thai *nak,* the mythological serpents to whose undersea realm Prince Sang sinks after the drowning attempt, have numerous elements in common with the Indian *nāgas,* both of Hinduism and of Buddhism. In Hindu mythology there are serpent-kings whose glittering capital is the glory of the underworld kingdom. They figure in many Buddhist *jātaka* tales, and are capable of appearing in human form and occupying palaces beneath the sea. In Hindu legends from the *Mahābhārata,* the *nāgas* cause men's death, and their favorite devices are surprise and trickery; in Buddhist legends, however, the help the *nāgas* extend to the Buddha, and indirectly to human beings, seems emphasized.

Within recent times in Thailand, midwives adjusted the body of a mother in labor to correspond to the supposed position of a certain *nak* under the earth, and thus make the birth less painful. To ensure the growth of their crops, Thai farmers have traditionally plowed the furrows of a field in the direction they believe a great *nak* to lie below their land.

The common element the serpent-king of *Sang Thong* has with these *nak* of Thai folk-belief and with the *nāgas* of Indian Hindu and Buddhist mythology is his power to influence men's lives. While similar in many respects to the *nāga* king of Hindu mythology, the serpent-king in *Sang Thong* more closely resembles the protective Buddhist figure. Like the *nak* of Thai folk-belief, the serpent-king in *Sang Thong* has the power to ease the suffering and ensure the sustenance of a human being.

ACT THREE

6. The Indian *garuda*, like the Thai *khrut*, is a mythological bird who is the enemy of the serpents. In a Theravada *jātaka* tale a *garuda* "swept up the water with the wind of its wings, and swooping down on the *nāga* region seized a *nāga* king by the head" ("Bhuridatta Jātaka" in E.B. Cowell, ed., *"The Jātaka": or Stories of Buddha's Former Births,* 6 vols. [Cambridge: Cambridge University Press, 1895–1907], 6:93).

The *khrut* is the symbol of the Thai king (though not in *Sang Thong*): the *garuda* is the transport of the god Vishnu.

7. The *yak* (ogres), as they are known in Thai, correspond to *yakkhā* (Pali masculine) and *yakkhiniyo* (Pali feminine). According to Malalasekera, *yakkha* had no negative connotation in early Buddhist records of the term. In later Buddhist literature, however, the *yakkha* were degraded and were described as red-eyed cannibal ogres, the female more to be feared than the male. Nevertheless, the attitude of the *yakkha* toward man in Buddhist literature is often one of benevolence (George P. Malalasekera, *Dictionary of Pali Proper Names,* 2 vols. [London: John Murray, 1937], 2: 676). This Buddhist conception seems very much that of the *yak* queen in *Sang Thong*. Although the *yak* are no longer spoken of as playing a part in human life in Thailand, their attribute of fierceness has added several expressions to the Thai language. Someone who kills another with no pity is said to have the heart of a *yak*.

8. The fortune-teller's prediction alludes to the folk tale *Rothasin* (also a dance-drama), in which Nang Meri, the daughter of an ogress, falls in love with the human Phra Rot. In the end he rides away from her, leaving her to die of a broken heart.

9. The ceremony called *somphot* is one traditionally per-

formed in Thailand to welcome an honored newcomer. In *Sang Thong*, the ogress's welcoming ceremony includes a *bai si* (literally, "auspicious rice"). On a tiered structure, food and sweetmeats are placed. The ceremony in *Sang Thong* also includes the act of *wian thian*, in which waving candles are carried or passed around the one who is wished well-being. (See Phya Anuman Rajadhon, *Essays on Thai Folklore* [Bangkok: Social Science Press of Thailand, 1968], pp. 218–33, for a fuller description of various types of *bai si* and of the act of *wian thian* as part of the *tham khwan* ceremony.)

10. The masked play (*khon*) is usually the *Ramakian* from the Indian *Ramayana*, in which the hero, Rama, with the help of the monkey band led by Hanuman, fights the demons. Mon dancing, which also formed part of the festivities at the welcoming ceremony for Prince Sang, had originated with the Mon people, whose state was once in Burma. Although the earliest Mon inscription in Thailand dates from the 7th or 8th century A.D., many of the Mon in Thailand at the time of Rama II were descendants of more recent refugees from Burma.

11. Negritos *(Ngaw)* live in the mountains of southern Thailand. With dark skin, kinky hair, and short stature, they are considered ugly by Thais. Transformations by which a demon or a divinity may appear as a man or a man may appear as an animal are common in Thai dramatic literature. However, Sang Thong's putting on of the Negrito form is not thought of by Thais as a transformation but simply as a disguise completely covering his body, rather like European armor. On stage, two different people take the parts of Sang Thong as the Negrito and Sang Thong as the prince. As the Negrito, the dancer wears a full head-mask.

ACT FOUR

12.   "Samon" is from the Pali *samanta* (neighboring, bordering). The area and its ruler both have the same name, Samon.

13.   Around each small rice plot there is a raised border to hold in the water. Prince Sang is sitting on one of these borders when the children find him.

ACT FIVE

14.   This expression, commonly used by Thais approaching old age, seems to indicate a very open recognition of the pains of aging.

15.   "Rochana" is from the Pali *rocana* (magnificent, splendid).

ACT SIX

16.   Bodily postures are often very expressive of feelings in Thai life, as well as in dance-dramas. Commonly, they express status deference of one person to another. Less commonly, a man who feels he has an unsolvable difficulty may sit on the floor with his arms around his knees drawn up to his chest, as King Samon does here. In a culture in which troubles are minimized, a child who sits in this way, copying someone in the household, may be urged that it is not a proper way to sit.

17.   Thai years, like Chinese ones, are named for animals. The even months are thought auspicious for marriages. The King was thus venting his anger at his daughter by having her live unwed with a man through this appropriate wedding month—a source of great shame.

18.   In the past a person angry with another, as Rochana's sisters are here, might pour out water and overturn a bowl

above it *(kruat nam khwam khan)*, signifying that he wanted never to meet the other person in this life or the next.

19. The idea of help that one has been given and should reciprocate *(bun khun)* occurs throughout *Sang Thong,* as it permeates traditional Thai values. Mrs. Maenmas Chavalit, head of the National Library, feels that the reason the episode of Prince Sang's leaving Phanthurat has been acted so infrequently is that, though Prince Sang recognizes Phanthurat's efforts to raise him, he leaves her heartbroken.

20. In the Thai New Year celebration, Songkran, city and country people pour water reverently on their priests and Buddha images, and gaily on each other, just as the Negrito pours water on Rochana here. Young people in the country play a game in which a bag full of seeds or nuts is thrown back and forth, and the Negrito tosses the utensil as if playing this game. (When anyone misses, in the Songkran country-game, he or she must leave the game and dance for the amusement of the remaining players.)

21. When Prince Sang says he comes from a kingdom beyond the sky, the cosmology suggested is of the sky, like an overturned bowl, covering the familiar world. Beyond the edges of the bowl live unknown human beings and other creatures.

22. The prince sings of the similarities between their love and that of Khun Phaen and Wanthong, who fled to the forest in the poetic story *Khun Chang Khun Phaen,* written by Sunthon Phu, one of Rama II's court poets. A note to the National Library edition of *Sang Thong* explains that this song was added to the dance-drama in the reign of King Chulalongkorn (Rama V).

ACT SEVEN

23. The lower garment *(panung)* traditionally worn by Thai women is a one-seamed tube of cloth, which is folded over to fit the wearer. Beneath the heavy belt used to hold it up, a woman who is particularly careful about her appearance may make pleated folds, as Rochana has done.

24. The verses the Negrito chants are from a *jātaka* story about Subin, a learned priest. A hunter who wished to give gifts of meat to the king figures in the song.

25. In Thai thought Prince Sang did not kill the fishes, which would be against Buddhist precepts, but only prayed for those who were about to die naturally to come up on the riverbank.

26. Thais may speak abusively to an animal or hit an object, as the king does here, when they are displeased with someone who is present.

27. This *phi khamot* (ghost or spirit) blamed by the men for their headaches is thought to live in the forest, causing trouble for men and animals. He has a black body.

28. Rochana's words to her older sister suggest a Thai feeling that, though the younger person owes the older one respect, the younger is not bound by the relationship if the older does not behave in a manner deserving respect.

29. The rest of this episode repeats the fishing incident, with similar details. I have included only those ideas and incidents which are new.

30. New robes are given to priests during a Kathin celebration.

ACT EIGHT

31. Traditionally Indra, or Phra In, as he is known to Thais, helps the good when they are in trouble. At such times

his soft-cushioned throne becomes hard. In Thai art, he is pictured as having green skin.

32. The description of the feelings of people concerned to save their lives and few possessions may reflect the early life of Rama II, when he lived as a commoner with his warrior father, during a period in which the new dynasty faced many threats.

33. Although the deity who here acts as the messenger of Indra is called Wisanukam, he is in fact the same figure respected by craftsmen in Thailand under the name Phra Wisawakam. In front of some Thai carpentry schools, a sculptured figure of Wisawakam holds a plumb line and tools. The modern Thai term for engineering is *wisawakam*.

34. *Ti khli* is an old Lao game played on foot across burned paddy fields in the evening. A ball that has been set on fire is hit into the air with a stick. Polo on horseback is an Indian and Western game.

35. For Thais, who have been taught how to pay respect to people of varied ranks from the time they were small children, the humor of the Negrito's awkwardness is particularly strong.

36. *Inao,* the entertainment promised by King Samon, was based on a story originating in Java and played as *lakhon nai* by the women of the court for many years before the writing of *Sang Thong* by Rama II.

ACT NINE

37. As James Mosel, among others, has noted, people in pre-modern Thailand rose and fell rapidly, depending on the favor of the king. (See Mosel's "Thai Administrative Behavior," in *Toward the Comparative Study of Public Administration,* ed. William J. Siffin [Bloomington: Indiana Univer-

sity Press, 1957].) People adapted readily to these changes in status, especially when a change, like that of the old couple in *Sang Thong,* brought them a higher position.

38. Although King Rama Khamheng in the Sukhothai era (A.D. 1275–1350) made it possible for any subject to petition him directly, later Thai kings in Ayutthaya acquired a semi-divine stature and were generally beyond access to all but a few courtiers. Yosawimon and Chanthewi risked arrest and imprisonment by approaching Prince Sang too directly.

Bibliography

Thai names follow the same order as English ones, but in Thailand the given name is used more frequently than the family name. (Dhanit Yupho, for example, is known as Professor Dhanit.) For this reason the given names of Thai authors, according to standard practice, precede their family names in this listing. With the exception of Phya, an untranslatable, conferred title, personal titles are given in translation.

Anuman Rajadhon (Phya): *Essays on Thai Folklore.* Bangkok: Social Science Press of Thailand, 1968.

Ayumongol Sonakul: "Understanding the Negrito: King Chulalongkorn's Efforts Result in a Play." *Standard: Bangkok Magazine,* October 27, 1968, pp. 12–14.

Bot Lakhon Khrang Krung Kao Rueang Nang Manora Lae Sang Thong [Scripts for Dance-Dramas from Former Times: *Manora* and *Sang Thong*], Bangkok: National Library, 1955.

Brandon, James R.: *Theatre in Southeast Asia.* Cambridge: Harvard University Press, 1967.

190   *Bibliography*

Chula Chakrabongse (Prince): *Lords of Life: A History of the Kings of Thailand.* London: Redman, 1960.

Cowell, E. B., ed.: *"The Jātaka": or Stories of Buddha's Former Births.* 6 vols. Cambridge: Cambridge University Press, 1895–1907.

Cuisinier, Jeanne: *Danses cambodgiennes.* Hanoi: Imprimerie d'Extrême-Orient, 1930.

Damrong Rachanuphap (Prince): *Phrarachaphongsawadan Krung Ratanakosin Ratchakan II* [History of the Reign of Rama II]. Bangkok: Samnakngan Siam Bannagan, 1929.

———: Introduction, *Panyasachatok* [Fifty Birth-Stories]. 2 vols. Bangkok: National Library, 1956.

———: Introduction, Phra Putthaloetla [King Rama II], *Bot Lakhon Nok Ruam 6 Rueang: Phrarachaniphon Ratchakan II* [Scripts for Six Dance-Dramas in the Style of Lakhon Nok, by King Rama II et al.]. Bangkok: National Library, 1958.

Dhanit Yupho: *The Khon and Lakon: Dance-Dramas Presented by the Department of Fine Arts.* Bangkok: Department of Fine Arts, 1963.

Dowson, John: *A Classical Dictionary of Hindu Mythology and Religion, Geography, History, and Literature.* 7th ed. London: Routledge and Kegan Paul, 1950.

Drans, Jean: *Histoire de Nang Manora et histoire de Sang Thong.* Tokyo: Presses Salesiennes, 1947.

Dwijendra Nath Neogi: *Sacred Tales of India.* London: Macmillan and Co., 1916.

Eliade, Mircea: *Myth and Reality.* Translated by Willard R. Trask. New York: Harper and Row, 1963.

Finot, Louis: "Recherches sur la littérature laotienne." *Bulletin de l'École Française d'Extrême-Orient* 17, no. 5 (1917): 1–128.

Hanks, Jane Richardson: *Maternity and its Rituals in Bang Chan*. Southeast Asia Program Data Paper no. 51. Ithaca, N.Y: Cornell University, 1962.

Larousse Encyclopedia of Mythology, New York: Prometheus Press, 1960.

Macdonald, Ariane: "La Naissance du monde au Tibet." In *La Naissance du monde*, Sources orientales, vol. 1. Paris: Éditions du Seuil, 1959.

The Mahāvastu. Translated from the Sanskrit by J. J. Jones. Vols. 16, 18, and 20 of *Sacred Books of the Buddhists*. London: Luzac and Co., 1949–56.

Malalasekera, George Peiris: *Dictionary of Pali Proper Names*. 2 vols. London: John Murray, 1937.

Mead, Margaret: "The Study of National Character." In *The Policy Sciences*. Edited by Daniel Lerner and Harold D. Lasswell. Stanford: Stanford University Press, 1951.

Montri Tramod: *Kanlalen Khawng Thai* [Thai Entertainment]. Bangkok: Phrachan, 1954.

Mosel, James: "Thai Administrative Behavior." In *Toward the Comparative Study of Public Administration*. Edited by William J. Siffin. Bloomington: Indiana University Press, 1957.

Nicholas, René: "Le Lakhon Nora ou lakhon chatri et les origines du théâtre classique siamois." *Journal of the Siam Society* 18, no. 2 (1924): 85–110.

Panyasachatok [Fifty Birth-Stories]. 2 vols. Bangkok: National Library, 1956.

Parker, Henry: *Village Folk-Tales of Ceylon*. 3 vols. London: Luzac and Co., 1910–14.

Phra Putthaloetla (King Rama II): *Bot Lakhon Nok Ruam 6 Rueang: Phrarachaniphon Ratchakan II* [Scripts for Six Dance-Dramas in the Style of *Lakhon Nok*, by King Rama

II et al.]. Bangkok: National Library, 1958.

Prem Purachatra (Prince): "Thai Literature: A Brief Survey." Seventh lecture in a series organized by the Thailand Council of the Asia Society, New York, N.Y., June, 1963. Mimeographed.

Redfield, Robert: *Peasant Society and Culture*. Chicago: The University of Chicago Press, 1956.

Snellgrove, David, and Richardson, Hugh: *A Cultural History of Tibet*. New York: Frederick A. Praeger, 1968.

Glossary-Index